First published in 2019 by Cool Springs Press, an imprint of The Quarto Group,
100 Cummings Center Suite 265D, Beverly, MA 01915 USA.
T (978) 282-9590 F (978) 283-2742 www.QuartoKnows.com



10 9 8 7 6 5 4 3 2 1

ISBN: 978-0-7603-6279-2

Digital edition published in 2019
eISBN: 978-0-7603-6280-8

Library of Congress Cataloging-in-Publication Data

Names: Colletti, Maria, 1959- author.
Title: Living decor : plants, potting and diy projects / Maria Colletti.
Description: Minneapolis, MN : Cool Springs Press, an imprint of
The Quarto Group, [2019] | Includes index.
Identifiers: LCCN 2018034479 | ISBN 9780760362792 (hc)
Subjects: LCSH: Interior landscaping. | House plants in interior decoration.
Classification: LCC SB419.25 .C65 2019 | DDC 635.9/65--dc23
LC record available at https://lccn.loc.gov/2018034479

Acquiring Editor: Alyssa Bluhm
Project Manager: Alyssa Lochner
Art Director: Cindy Samargia Laun
Cover and Page Design: Amelia LeBarron

Printed in China

Plants, Potting and DIY Projects

# LIVING DECOR

Botanical Styling with Fiddle-Leaf Figs, Monsteras, Air Plants, Succulents, Ferns, and More of Your Favorite Houseplants

MARIA COLLETTI

# CONTENTS

# INTRODUCTION

**HELLO, MY HOUSEPLANT-LOVING FRIENDS!** Let's go on a trip to a new kind of jungle: a land created with gorgeous indoor landscapes that are so green; a place where we love to live with our houseplants daily in every room.

All our living plants, our indoor greenery, speak a universal language of green. Social media has taken us everywhere from Australia, Brazil, and Scandinavia to moss-loving Japan. Millennials and baby boomers alike are creating worlds of urban jungles and tropical homes. We want to whet our appetites for the new modern "it" houseplants, large plants such as the fiddle-leaf fig and *Monstera*. Plants are sharing spaces with us and our pets. Social media brings inspirational visions by people popularizing this style to our laptops and phones, then we stop by our local marketplaces to buy these green wonders to carry home.

Surround yourself with greenery in multiple styles of plants until you feel a real, honest love of nature and plants. Modern indoor greenery is a source of living decor inspiration.

This is nature's botanical-styling perfection.

All over our homes and work areas, plants can be styled creatively to share spaces with us and our pets. Plants of all sizes, climates, species, and colors can be displayed in geometric-shaped terrariums, mid-century pots, or flea-market finds.

In a world of ever-increasing electronic dependence, it has become paramount to our very existence to have plants close to our hearts, to watch them grow, to lovingly tend them and immerse our lives right in the natural.

Botanical styling has become part of our culture and everyday life. As a highly visual person, I notice many details in a room, a garden, or on the roadside. When I watch a movie or television program, I always notice the plants in the background: a terrarium in the room, the pot of succulents or the cloche on the coffee table, or the windowsill full of houseplants. One commercial for Keurig coffee makers with James Corden, host of *The Late Late Show*, had me belly laughing. James is going on about how everyone should be ditching their glass coffee pots for the new Keurig coffee maker. He illustrates this hilariously by holding up a glass coffee pot full of plants and proclaims, "Look, it's a terrarium!" Yeah, baby, terrariums go mainstream!

*Living Decor* is a modern indoor greenery guide of inspiration and ideas, a visual photographic show, a step-by-step instruction manual, and an indoor houseplant guide. This book will help you take care of your rising urban jungle or tropical houseplant revolution by teaching you how to design and create your own botanical style with today's houseplants, preserved moss art, chandelier gardens, succulents, terrariums, and hanging glass globes filled with air plants, moss, and more.

We will channel through today's trends in living with plants with macramé hanging plant holders and concrete planters that show how beautiful, unique, creative, and even artistic displays with plants can be. We all want to replicate garden shop displays as we bring plants we can't resist into our own spaces and overpopulate our bookshelves. Here, I share styling ideas from my favorite shopkeepers, where I find my inspiration. I offer you pictures to drool over, and instruction on how to create these wonderful displays we so want to covet. This book will guide you through buying, planting, and caring for the living decor displays you will create.

Being a designer, a crafter, and a maker entails creative stepping stones:

- Ideas: actual design concept
- Inspirations: what ideas do you find fuel your creative process
- Trends: what's popular now
- Suppliers: how to find materials
- Project: how to achieve your vision
- Marketplace: how do shops display
- Interpretation: the result of your artistic vision

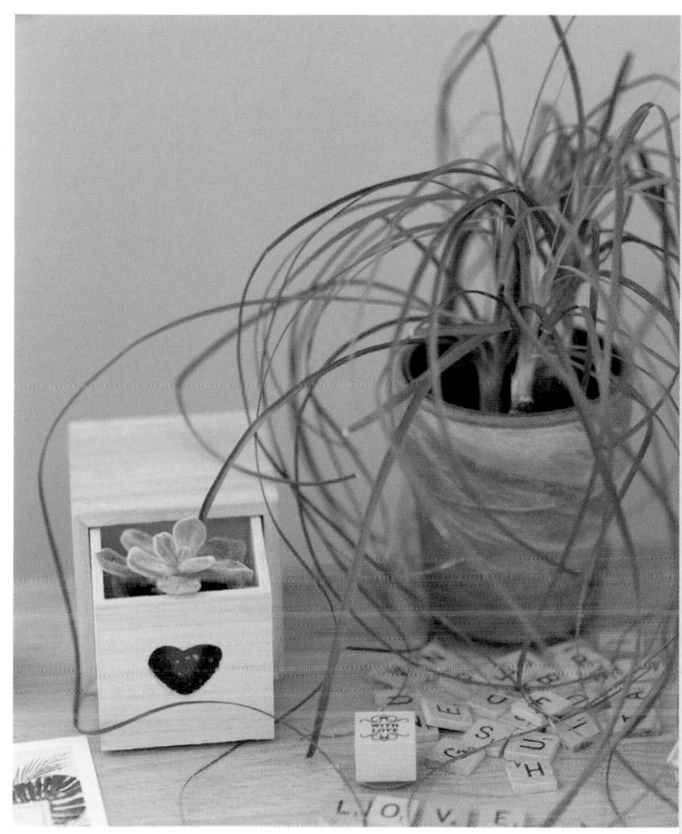

Elements of a crafter's desk include the fruits of creative projects.

## WHERE I FOUND MY GREEN LIFE

New York Botanical Garden is a place I had only dreamed I'd be able to work someday. So, when I started right out of horticulture school in a summer gardening program, I was thrilled it was really happening. I later returned to work for NYBG at a small, precious gem of a plant shop in the IBM atrium on Madison Avenue. We would create displays in the windows and spend our days replacing trays of plants and cacti from the downstairs stockroom. Those days were fun and I was learning the plant shop business. In 2003, I continued my schooling at NYBG, chiseling my green skills as shop manager of the Shop in the Garden. The shop included books, ceramics, wonderful garden supplies, gorgeous pillows, and custom-designed fern dinnerware. When my first book, *Terrariums: Gardens under Glass*, was published, I had the honor of being interviewed by a wonderful reporter for *Edible Manhattan*, who crowned me the "terrarium savant."

I learned so much working as a garden retailer in a place that educates daily on what it means to love plants. We bought, sold, displayed, and cared for our plant inventory. We watched the garden evolve throughout the seasons, which was, on many days, just breathtaking: the white Korean dogwood trees at the entrance of the rose garden, or the perennial garden outside the Enid A. Haupt Conservatory in summer. My gratitude is massive. How lucky am I? I intended never to waste this privilege but instead utilize it to the best of my abilities. This is how I discovered my garden lifestyle and brought all the elements together.

I spent thirteen years at the NYBG shop creating displays with plants and other merchandise to produce endless visual scenes to entice our plant-loving shoppers and thousands of tourists per year. Every year, a new theme arose from the cycle of plant exhibits created in the Enid A. Haupt Conservatory. The gardens of artists were recreated under the giant glass dome, including the wildly successful Frida Kahlo garden exhibit, the inspired Emily Dickinson herbarium collection, and a replica of the moon gate of the Abby Aldrich Rockefeller Garden in Seal Harbor, Maine. Did you know that Monet chose all those water lilies himself in his paintings? Each exhibit was different, and each time I learned something new about plants from the gardens and lives of each extraordinary artist.

I've learned to bring my love for plant displays home with me. I create stories on my windowsills, on my coffee table, on my shelves, and in my bedroom. I live in an ever-changing snapshot of my life—past, present, and the next big influence that inspires me to create a place at home that reminds me of all my collective experiences.

## THE WORKSHOP & ITS INSTRUCTOR

I always wanted to be an instructor at the New York Botanical Garden. I placed the instructors and garden curators at NYBG on a high pedestal of the elite garden world because they are. I would listen to the orchid curator speak about and spell the names of hundreds of rare orchid genera and species. Quite impressive! My expectations for myself were just as high off the ground. For years, I avoided considering the idea of teaching, but I was going to find a subject or an idea that was worthy of it. Perseverance! In 2010 began the decade of the terrarium revival and I found my skill, my design sense, and my first reason to attempt teaching.

I gave this teaching idea a chance by selling the idea of a terrarium workshop to the director of the Bronxville Adult School, Barbara Corcoran. She said yes, she loved the idea, and she believed people were ready to start playing with terrariums. The day of my first class, I was petrified that I would stumble over every word. I perceived myself to be awful that night, but two women stayed after class to chat and clean up. Okay, maybe it wasn't a complete disaster.

So, I kicked myself into gear. I learned PowerPoint to give presentations because terrariums are a visual as well as a hands-on learning experience. By then, it was the age of social media, so I opened five social media accounts and created a website. This took months, and before I knew it, two years had gone by and the head of the adult education department at NYBG was none other than Barbara Corcoran from Bronxville. Barbara remembered me, and at that point, terrariums had begun to rev up in popularity. She and I collaborated, and I signed up to teach a class for the next season.

I think it's important to admit how nervous we humans can get when embarking on something new. It's a natural experience, but it still gave me stage fright. I kept telling myself people like the uber-famous Carly Simon and Barbra Streisand both have lived with stage fright and have managed successful careers. What would they do in my situation? My hands shook and my stomach turned. Normal, right?

For weeks prior to my first class at NYBG, I lay awake at night thinking about standing in front of a class of students who, I imagined, expected an instructor at NYBG to be all-knowing. The day finally came and I prepared all day, went over my PowerPoint slides, and drove to the school. Then something magical happened . . .

At the end of the class, the students thanked me profusely and left happily, bouncing out the door with their own new prized creations. The joy on their faces only rivaled what I was feeling inside. This act of teaching turned out to be more enjoyable for me than I had ever imagined it could be. Seeing those happy, grateful faces is why I love being a workshop instructor.

After five years, my nerves have calmed and I work to improve with each class. My small beginning has led me to more lectures and demonstrations and given me the confidence to speak for garden clubs in New Canaan, Connecticut; Sands Point, Long Island; and at *Country Living Magazine*'s Fair in Rhinebeck, New York, where I was a featured presenter. At the beginning of each class, I thank the students for taking my class because, as I say, without them, there would be no me, and I remind them how much I will also learn from them. Their imagination is infinite.

A dream realized is a life well spent. This is how and where I found my green life to create terrariums and display houseplants, books, favorite objects, and all things a garden lifestyle can explore. My motto has always been that collaboration promotes inspiration for all! So, this book is a labor of my plant love, a love that I hope brings you years of joy as it has for me. Happy houseplanting!

# I.

# THE GREENERY

**PLANTS MAKE PEOPLE HAPPY.** This is how I feel about plants—*my* plants. How wonderful to have a part of nature in your life that invokes happiness. Happiness is warm, pleasant love. This invokes the philosophy that it *is* the simple things in life that make us happy.

Let me elaborate. My indoor garden designs and my indoor plant choices follow that simple philosophy. Happiness can be a place, a time, a memory, an idea, or a feeling we remember when we gaze at our surroundings and the objects we choose to own.

In my world, nature is my happy place. I need a walk in the woods to see the ferns breaking through the ground in spring. I need a stroll on the beach where I pick up prized seashells for my collection. I enjoy a moment sitting on a rock, gazing at the lakeside, where a breeze blows gently. I feel myself breathe out slowly when I drive down a country road by a pasture full of sheep.

Mismatched pots and lush green life pop out against a stark white background. Who wouldn't feel at home in this room?

This collection of plants is provided by Amelie Segrestan of My Little Greens, a Brooklyn-based succulent-design company.

I also enjoy the urban adventure of people racing through concrete streets, and bustling vendors in a historic part of town selling their handmade crafts. On any day, you can take a self-guided neighborhood walking tour and gawk up at amazing architecture.

Let's combine that which we covet. I enjoy city life, country life, and everything in between. Filling our living and working spaces with nature, with memories, and with those objects that evoke a warm feeling reminds us of what we love. I call it *snapshots of our lives*.

# SNAPSHOTS OF OUR LIVES

When I create living decor displays, I combine all those objects that give me joy. This includes my favorite plant, which I have tended for years and watched grow into a healthy green specimen. I include found objects such as shells from that wonderful summer I spent on Florida's Sanibel Island beach, my favorite vintage armillary I found while antiquing in the Catskill Mountains, and, of course, my favorite books.

The houseplant has risen to its glory days again. Plants can reduce dry skin by increasing humidity indoors, which makes us look and feel healthier. Plants also purify our air indoors, which improves our respiratory comfort. In the workplace, plants can increase our feelings of wellness, and have been credited with reducing stress and increasing productivity. When we are calmer and happier, our minds are free to be creative. These are pretty impressive accomplishments by our green friends.

This corner of my desk demonstrates what I call display mixology: a mix of plants with some of my favorite objects.

# WHAT IS DISPLAY MIXOLOGY?

*Display mixology* is what I call my design style. It includes a still-life portrait of objects living and nonliving, creating a place, time, or season that visually inspires that feeling, that spark of joy.

My style always includes an object with living plants, whether in a terrarium, as a topiary, or an air plant. Here they all are!

This magnificent room at photographer Lori Adams's studio gave me a playground to create this seasonal mixology. Lori has her framed photographs lined up in a wall display. On the table you see air plants, English ivy (right), and colorful spears of *Croton* (left) mixing with pumpkins and gourds. On the shelves, I added cylindrical terrariums, heart-shaped frames filled with moss, and lights for that twinkle. I love to add lights inside terrariums, in displays, and strung up on shelves all year round. In each section of this book, you will learn how to create these elements and how to put them together. Let's find inspiration together page by page as the story unfolds.

I created all the displays in this book with attention to each detail, layering plants and memorabilia with a touch of love. This is my passionate pursuit and it is hardly work because I love creating small scenes of joy. Give me a blank space or surface and I will fill it with botanicals and living decor. For me, display is infectious and I never tire of creating another story. Join the club!

## GENERAL PLANT CARE TIPS

Greet your plants every day like you'd greet your children, partners, and pets. As their caretaker, ask yourself what their needs are today. A plant's three most important basic needs are light, water, and care. Once you have the basics, you will find it easier to keep your jungle green and healthy. If your greenery is happy, then you are happy. Here are some basic plant care tips.

### LIGHT

Our green plants need sunlight to grow healthy and remain green. Photosynthesis is how our plants create life and in turn create life for us. When explained that way it becomes immediately profound how much we need greenery to sustain us.

Simple factors dictate the intensity of the sun, such as direction of sunlight and time of day. Is it winter or summer, and how long is the daylight where you live? Are you above or below the Equator? Your locale predicts humidity, sun intensity, or the length of winters—it marks the difference between living in Brazil or Canada.

Succulents in particular will grow leggy without enough light intensity. In the Northeast, I supplement my succulents with a clip-on spotlight attached to my plant stand. When I'm home, I turn it on and they struggle a bit less to grab the light, especially during winter. Even a normal, everyday lamp can supplement light indoors.

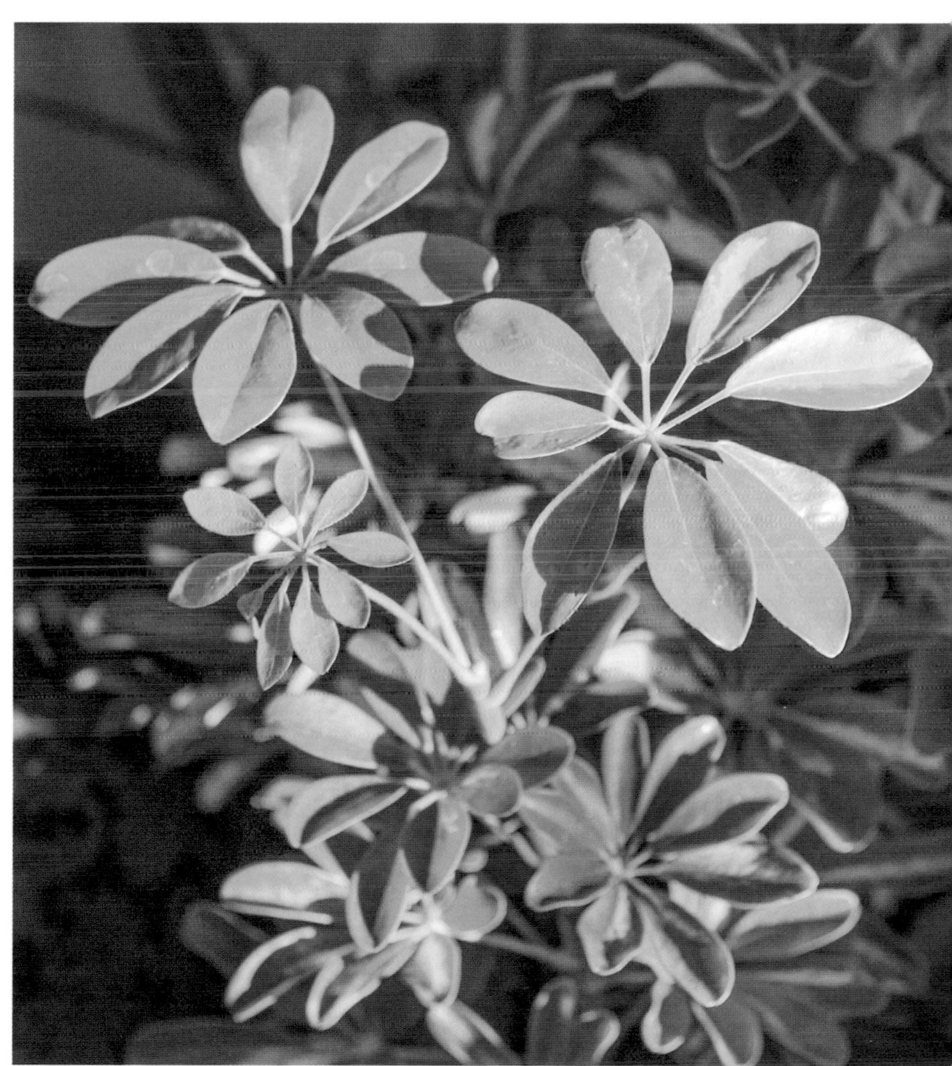

*Arboricola* in sunlight.

In what direction does your window face? East light is strong and direct in the morning, which gives plants a good bath of light. *Phalaenopsis* orchids prefer it. Southern windows offer a longer bath of light from late morning to late afternoon and can be very hot around noon. Western windows are hot into the evening in summer, so choose plants that can handle hot summer sun for hours. North windows receive the least amount of natural light.

*Indirect light* is a term often mentioned as a crowd-pleasing light requirement for many houseplants. Of course, what it means is up for interpretation per your individual indoor environment, such as whether trees obstruct the light of your south-facing window. Once you establish the sufficiency of your environmental parameters, then your plant care will follow.

## PHOTOSYNTHESIS

Photosynthesis is the process by which green plants use sunlight to convert carbon dioxide and water into energy, then release oxygen as a byproduct into the atmosphere. Photosynthesis involves chlorophyll, the green pigment in leaf cells. The process always begins when chlorophyll absorbs energy from light. Plants turn toward the sun for nourishment, which in turn helps them grow new leaves.

It is very important to rotate your living decor, whether it includes houseplants, terrariums, hanging baskets, tabletop gardens, or trailing plants on bookshelves. Indoor plants turn toward the sunlight provided for them. They bend and twist to reach that precious light coming in the window. Plant growth in the direction of a light source is called *positive phototropism*.

If plants only receive sunlight to one side for an extended period of time, they can become spindly, weak, or irregularly shaped. To avoid this, rotate your plants often. This will help them grow full and lush on all sides.

## THRESHOLD WATERING

As we water our plants, we take a break from the rigors of the day. When I care for my plants, I aim for consistency and healthy responses using what I call *factors of threshold watering*. When a plant's leaves or stems are stiffly pointing upward, I know they are at their maximum healthiness. I would rather my plants not develop brown or yellow leaves, and I don't like drooping plants or soggy soil. I strive to find that sweet spot with my watering where the plants maintain green, upright leaves and the soil holds a moderate amount of moisture at all times. It keeps the plants at their maximum health.

There are three easy considerations for creating your plant's threshold watering gap:

- What kind of plant is it?
- What direction is the light or heat source?
- Is the water able to drain freely through the soil?

So, what plant are you watering? If it is a maidenhair fern (*Adiantum*) or peace lily (*Spathiphyllum*), you can practically sit each of these plants in a dish of water. Both of these plants love having moist soil and usually can't get enough water. If you have an *Agave* or spiny *Opuntia* cactus, then you need to let the soil dry thoroughly, meaning deeper than just the top of the soil. The watering schedule or gap between watering is created by the plant itself. Can it tolerate only a few days going without water, or two weeks? Answering that question will get you closer to figuring out your watering threshold.

Light and/or heat sources can also affect the watering threshold. What is the location of your plant? Is it directly on the windowsill, on a table away from windows, near a heat source such as the kitchen, or under an intense desk lamp? This will affect the plant's water usage and the timing of your next watering. If plants live in your kitchen, the heat from cooking will dry out the soil faster. If your plant sits in a cool room that does not

### FACTORS OF THRESHOLD WATERING

How do you figure out the threshold watering needs of your plant? When the soil in a houseplant's pot goes too dry for the plant living in that pot, the plant will lose green color and turn yellow. This is your plant's cry for water. If there is a brown leaf, then the soil is so dry that there is little for the plant to drink up into the leaf, so the leaf turns brown. Monitor your watering intervals to discover your plant's water threshold; for example, if you have been watering every seven days and a leaf turns brown, then try watering every five days. Close the gap between watering so the soil will not dry out past what the potted plant will tolerate.

receive direct sunlight, a plant will most likely be able to go longer between watering, as it simply will not utilize as much water.

The last factor is whether water properly drains through the pot. Does the pot have drainage holes or is it in a decorative outer pot? I often take my smaller pots to the sink and run water through the pot, then let them sit there on a rack until the last drop of water drips out the bottom of the pot.

If you cannot move the plant, then make sure it has an ample-sized plant saucer, cup, or plate to sit upon. Layering some gravel in the saucer will raise the pot and allow extra water to travel below the gravel and away from the roots of the plant. It also creates an air pocket to help excess water evaporate.

If you have a palm, fiddle-leaf fig, or a plant with flat, leathery leaves that can withstand a nice, warm rain shower, then feel free to sit your plants in the shower for two to three minutes. Allow the water to fall softly so as not to damage the leaves or branches. Let the water be slightly warm, especially if the plant has dried severely or if it is the middle of winter, when indoor heating has a drying effect on leaves. This is a good practice once every six months.

OPPOSITE: Watering my tropical *Monstera* and fiddle-leaf fig plants in the shower helps to recreate their humid native climates.

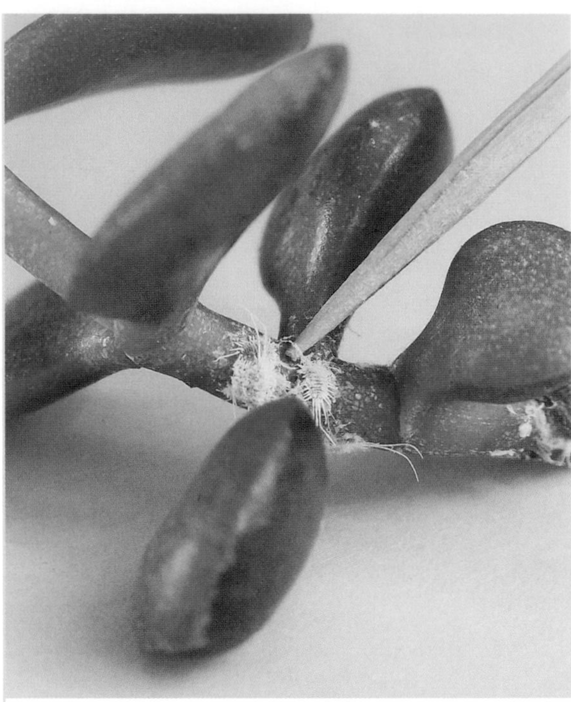

ABOVE: Hungry mealy bugs love to hide in the crevices of jade plants.

BELOW: Spider mites are minuscule orange or red bugs.

## CARE

I refer to the care of a plant as the extra essentials that will contribute to the overall health and attractive growth of your plants. For example, pruning is an essential care that your plants will occasionally need.

### PRUNING

Vines require a snip at the end to keep them strong and bushy. Anyone who has let their *Pothos* trail along for yards and yards without ever giving it a haircut will tell you it got kind of scrawny. A haircut is exactly how you should think about pruning. Pruning will properly keep a plant's growth pattern attractive and will help the plant concentrate its growth efforts not only on the tip of the stem but on the entire plant.

### INSECTS

Watching for insects is an important care task. Take a closer look at the stems and undersides of your plant's leaves every once in a while, especially if the plant is looking tired and wilted. It could just need water, or maybe it has some bug taking advantage of its good health.

**Mealy bugs** are particularly hurtful. They are small white bugs that grow in colonies and look like cotton in the crevice of a stem. Mealy bugs love jade plants (*Crassula*)—when I catch even just one mealy bug, I leap into action. I take the plant into the bathroom, where I dip a cotton swab into rubbing alcohol and remove the bug with it. Then I wash the plant itself with some warm water, covering the pot in a plastic bag so as not to let the water wash through the soil. This usually works for me, but it's important to stay visually alert to any more bugs coming your way.

**Spider mites** love palms, umbrella plants, English ivy, and other plants that sit in strong sun exposure indoors. The heat and sun create a breeding ground for spontaneous generation. Spider mites seem to mysteriously arrive on the scene and appear out of nowhere, but once they make their way onto the underside of the palm fronds or finger leaves of an umbrella plant, they can do their damage. The top side of the leaf will look mottled. To combat this, you will want to add some drops of dish soap to a spray bottle filled with water and mist the plant, especially the underside of the leaves, with soapy water. It helps to deprive the bugs of a breeding ground and they eventually diminish. If the plant is fairly large, you should place a drop cloth on the floor, then spray, spray, spray. Plants should be sprayed every two weeks with the soapy solution as a general practice to prevent any mites from getting ahead of you.

**Fungus gnats** are those pesky, small black bugs flying around your plant, its soil, and your living space. Gnats like moisture and they love moist soil—which is where they live. If you start to notice them a lot and you are able to cut back on watering your plants, they sometimes disappear or die off. But often, they leave offspring behind in the soil to invade your space once they hatch. If the gnats really become a nuisance, take the plant out of the pot and discard the soil outside. Then wash the pot with hot, soapy water, clean the old soil off the roots of the plant, and re-plant in a clean, new environment. This is the most effective solution.

ABOVE: I love letting my spider plants grow long, but be sure to prune yours to keep them out of reach of nibbling pets.

BELOW: One little leaf scrap was enough to lure all these gnats into this sticky tape trap.

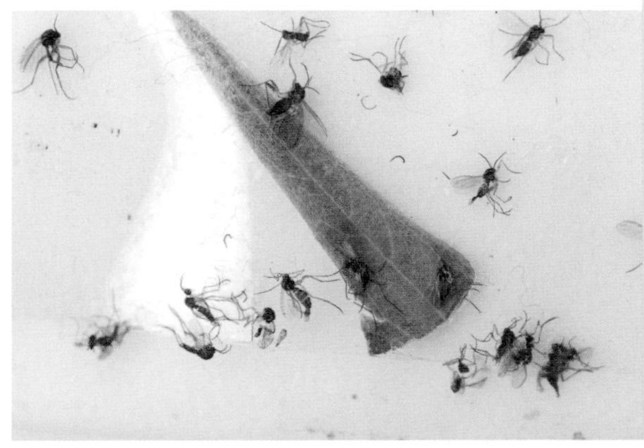

LOVE ♡
BIG LOVE
PLANT LOVE
#MONSTERA
MONDAY
HOUSE PLANTS
HOW TO LOOK AFTER
YOUR INDOOR PLANTS
WITH HELPFUL ADVICE,
STEP-BY-STEP PROJECTS, AND
INVENTIVE PLANTING IDEAS

# THE HOUSEPLANT REINVENTED

Let's talk about some of those fabulous tropical houseplants we are lining up to include in our own oases. These are the wonderful "it" plants and we simply cannot get enough of their wild tropical beauty.



OPPOSITE: My letterboard tells it all about my big plant love!

# FICUS LYRATA (FIDDLE-LEAF FIG)

The versatile fiddle-leaf fig is an interior designer's dream plant, a photo stylist-preferred prop. The world-renowned, the one, the only, the fabulous "it" plant of every furniture catalog from IKEA to Crate & Barrel. Let me introduce you to the fiddle-leaf fig. That's its common name; the botanical name is *Ficus lyrata*.

The fiddle-leaf is easy to care for. If you give this plant the proper lighting and water, it won't ask for another thing. Mine has been with me for about eight years now; I rescued it from someone else's dumpster. After a summer or two outside on a covered deck, where it would get soakings from the garden hose, I was concerned it would not acclimate to my apartment living room, but it is doing great. With new leaves making it a foot taller and growing more each year, I believe it will reach the ceiling one day. How do I keep my fiddle-leaf fig alive and growing?

The leaf of a fiddle-leaf fig has a strong, leathery feel. It is durable and can be cleaned to a polished shine with a bit of soapy water and a clean sponge.

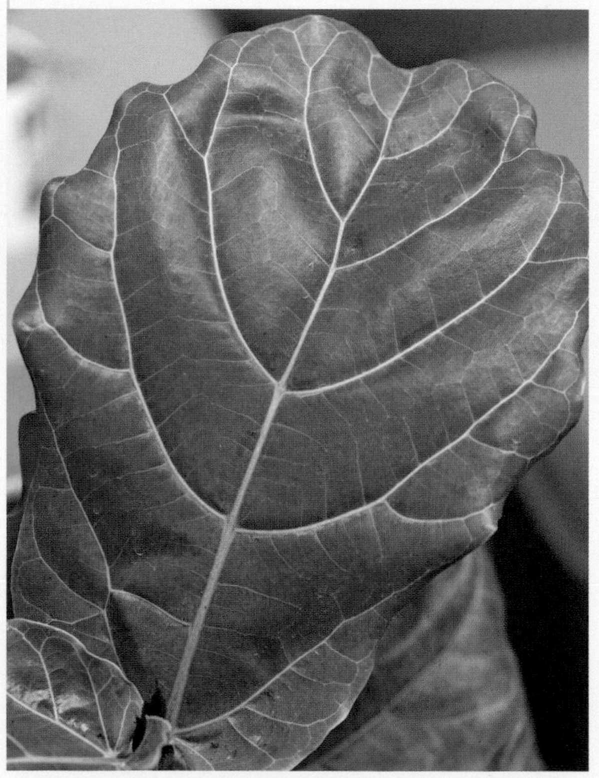

## LIGHT

Fiddle-leaf figs like a good light source. My plant lives in front of two windows. The front window gets strong morning sunrays, which bathe my fiddle-leaf, and then the indirect sun moves around to its left side as the sun moves through the sky. During the year, I turn the tall plant round and round so it will grow straight and not crooked. Both direct and indirect sunlight are good things.

## WATER

Fiddle-leaf will only drop a leaf if the available water in the soil has evaporated past its threshold. Remember, seasons change available sunlight. In areas of the world where the sun sets early in the day in winter, fiddle-leaf may hold water longer. Where the sun beats strong all day, a fiddle-leaf will need a good soaking until the water drains all the way through the bottom of the pot.

I sometimes drag my darling plant into the shower, which is a challenge now that it has grown to five feet tall. I leave

A nice, warm shower now and then is a good thing. It washes the dust off the leaves and lets the water drain completely through the soil.

it in the shower for a while, close the bathroom door, and let the humidity gather. If this task seems ridiculous, that's understandable—it's easier to take a damp cloth and gently wipe the dust off the large, veined leaves.

## DESIGN MIXOLOGY

The fiddle-leaf has become so popular that plant suppliers are now flooding the marketplace with different sizes to fit every spot in your space. A plant with one trunk-like stem is often referred to as topiary; a plant with several woody stems can be a bush. Garden shops and centers sell different heights, ranging from smaller, three-foot versions to large, treelike plants standing at six feet tall. Of course, the larger the plant, the more expensive it is.

Consider the spot you intend to place your fiddle-leaf. In most situations, you will see the fiddle-leaf rising from behind a couch in a living room setting or adjacent to a chair or bed. It is part of the decor and should be placed accordingly. The larger single-stem but multi-branched fiddle-leaf can fill a corner spot. My large specimen stays on the same side of the room and I shift it season to season. In summer, it needs to be shielded from the window's powerful air conditioner, and in winter it needs to move closer to the window's light.

## *MONSTERA DELICIOSA* (SWISS CHEESE PLANT)

The botanical name describes how we feel about this plant: *Monstera deliciosa*. What isn't delicious about *Monstera*? Everyone must have one—must! It has popped onto the plant scene with ferocity and abundance. Affectionately, *Monstera* is called swiss cheese plant or split-leaf philodendron, which describes the natural cuts in its massive, glossy leaves (*Monstera* is not actually a philodendron, which is a separate genus). *Monstera* looks like it would be an Amazon Jungle plant, so I was surprised to read it actually originates from Southern Mexico into Central America (Southern Mexico is a more humid terrain, where lots of heat rises). In its native habitat, *Monstera* will grow fruit, hence its name, *deliciosa*, but it likely won't fruit indoors.

An unfurling *Monstera* leaf.

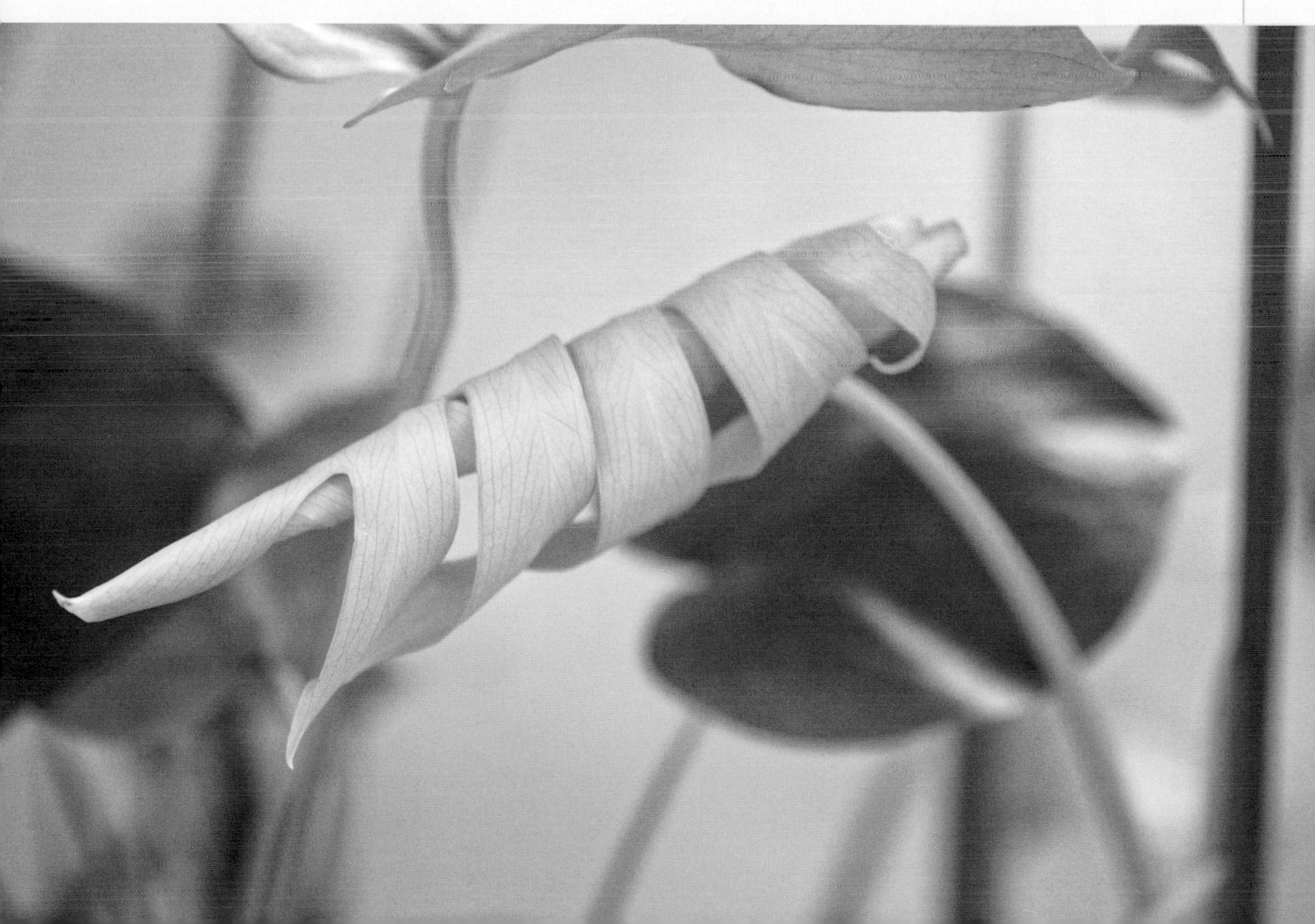

## LIGHT

In a jungle, plants residing in the understory receive dappled light. Remember, jungle understory light is still much stronger than indoor sunlight. *Monstera* can withstand a bright, sunny window as long as you provide water to keep it from severely drying out. You will not want to expose it to all-day hot sun, say in Arizona or California, but bright light is okay.

## WATER

Your *Monstera*'s soil should go until slightly dry to the touch before watering. When you water, try to find a way to water thoroughly with proper drainage—then you can go a bit longer between watering. Remember to keep the leaves free of dust and bugs by wiping them with a damp cloth. Occasionally misting with room-temperature water will increase its intake of moisture on the leaves and will create a more humid environment. *Monstera* is a vine and will need a pinch or two as the plant grows to keep its shape and strength.

## DESIGN MIXOLOGY

*Monstera* has brown aerial roots, which help them hold on to adjoining trees in the jungle—so, at home, your plant will need room to spread its branching arms. While it is excellently on display wherever you can look down onto those magnificent leaves, you may be able to sit your *Monstera* on a plant stand or stool to spare it from damage as you walk around them. *Monstera* can thrive while growing upright on a wooden stake, or gangly and reaching out in all directions. You will need an ample spot for your *Monstera* so you do not constantly hit the leaves, as they will tear. If you see roots poking out the bottom of the pot in a year or so, that is a signal to repot to the next size up and add some new, rich potting soil. Let your *Monstera* flourish, because #MonsteraMondays never get you down!

Brooklyn lounges comfortably on #MonsteraMonday. The nearby *Monstera*'s robust jungle leaves are clean, healthy, and shiny. Our lounging model knows she has the best spot in her home. Brooklyn does not nibble on the plant, so her mom, Meagan, can trust her to lounge around it.

#CALATHEALOVERS

# CALATHEA LANCIFOLIA (RATTLESNAKE PLANT)

Rattlesnake plant, or *Calathea lancifolia*, is very lovely. Its long, sword-shaped leaves with purple undersides and green topsides are ornamented with slender, dark green markings that fan out from the center veins. Each sword swirls out from the soil, creating many stems shooting upward. Living plants are so intricate in their appearances. How can this be real? This species has many variations; you will want to collect the entire *Calathea* genus.

Not to be outdone by *C. lancifolia*, *C. orbifolia* is commonly called peacock plant because its leaf markings resemble a peacock's tail markings. Its alternating green-gray lines radiate from the center vein. *C. orbifolia* has a unique growth style, sending up round, orb-shaped leaves. As each leaf grows in maturity, the color can change from lighter to darker shades, but it is the height of each stem that creates a bushy plant. I adore this plant!

Beautiful *Calathea lancifolia*.

## LIGHT

It is highly suggested that you keep your *Calathea* from very hot sun or bright direct light, which could scorch its leaves. This plant will let you know if the sun is too hot by curling its leaves. Keep it away from cold windows in winter. Please do not use leaf shine products; they can ruin those lovely leaves.

## WATER

*Calathea* is native to Brazil, which has a moist, humid climate. To duplicate that environment, you can sit the pot on a pebble tray or saucer with a bit of water. If you want to elevate your caretaking, buy a humidifier. You and your plants will breathe better. Keep the soil evenly moist but not waterlogged, and do not let the soil dry out completely. You can taper back slightly during winter's shorter days. If you ignore your specimen for weeks and weeks, the leaves will shrivel and the plant

might die. *Calathea* has a delicate sheerness to its leaves and can be susceptible to brown tips when dryness takes over. If browning occurs, you may slice off the tips with a pair of sharp scissors. Do your best to keep the soil evenly moist, something this beautiful specimen needs.

## DESIGN MIXOLOGY

*Calathea lancifolia* is a graceful plant with many color options to match your decor. The leaf underside is a striking solid plum. You could create an entire interior design scheme around the rattlesnake plant. Buy a mission-style cherry wood stand and place your rattlesnake plant prominently atop it against a backdrop of velvet plum drapes. Then match the couch in green velvet to complement the topside of the leaves. I see it coming together as an extravagant, luxuriant parlor. You and your *Calathea* deserve it.

The idea here is to use your plants to either complement your room decor already in place or let nature dictate to you a color combination you may never have considered.

*C. orbifolia* is consistently green and will fit in well with your entire houseplant jungle. Its small stature can sit decoratively on any surface. Don't crowd it with other plants and hide it from view, so you have full access to those special peacock-like leaves. Also, crowding plants together creates the possibility that *C. orbifolia* will be shaded. *C. orbifolia* can sit as a single specimen because of its interesting markings.

# *PILEA PEPEROMIOIDES* (CHINESE MONEY PLANT)

#CHINESEMONEYPLANT

*Pilea peperomioides*, known as Chinese money plant, is a species native to southern China. You may hear it called pancake plant, which refers to the plant's flat, round green leaves. *Pilea peperomioides* was practically not available in America until recently, when the houseplant jungle revolution arrived on the scene. It was so rare that plant suppliers began to propagate it at home in order to keep up with demand—it's common to see plant supplier sites state that supply is limited. The resource section in the back of this book will list suppliers where you can check for inventory, and prices vary with availability. So, literally, get the pancake plant while it's still hot!

*Pilea peperomioides* requires very basic care. It is an easy plant and adapts to low-light environments. It even accepts cooler rooms in winter, which may encourage it to bloom tiny white flowers. *Pilea* is a strong species; its leathery leaves are not delicate to the touch and do not wilt easily.

The Chinese money plant in various stages of growth.

## LIGHT

You should provide bright, indirect light and shield the plant from direct sun so the leaves don't burn. Remember to respond to your light conditions according to season and time of day. Don't burn the leaves in the summer's scorching sun.

## WATER

*Pilea peperomioides* likes regular watering, which translates to this: If you see droopy leaves, check to see if it dried out past its threshold tolerance. You will need to use a pot with holes so the excess water drains out. Maybe keep a calendar on the wall and log when you water until the plant's stems are standing up at attention. Then you know they have enough water.

## DESIGN MIXOLOGY

*Pilea peperomioides* will easily mix in with your green jungle against white walls. Its unique structure will bring variety to the shape of your jungle too. *Pilea* will tolerate sitting on an east-facing windowsill that cools down at night. The plant grows slowly and therefore can sit on a table where it does not take up much room. You can flaunt your hard-won treasure with other prized collections. This will make your neighboring plant pal green with envy!

OPPOSITE: *Pilea* fits right in with these other popular houseplants in coordinating black and white pots.

*#SANSEVIERIASUNDAY*

# *SANSEVIERIA TRIFASCIATA* (SNAKE PLANT)

The sturdy, durable, un-killable snake plant has been around forever. I bet your great-grandmother had one. My dog chewed on one of mine when I was a child and the plant kept going strong. Today, growers are bringing new species and varieties to the marketplace—common ones include *Sansevieria trifasciata* 'Laurentii', which is edged with gold, and 'Hahnii', a dwarf variety. My favorite is *S. cylindrica*. The plant has tall, hard, upward spears, and some suppliers carry them with their many stems braided together.

## LIGHT

Indoor snake plants are very tolerant of low- to no-light situations; they are often used in office buildings for this reason. Still, all plants need some light source—this plant will accept filtered or fluorescent light. Ceiling lights left on for hours or a supplemental lamp near the plant will substitute well if there is a lack of natural light or no window nearby.

## WATER

Let the soil of the *Sansevieria* dry out between watering. They really do not need much care, and their legendary reputation of being indestructible is well founded. Snake plants are technically succulents and can be planted in cactus soil, which contains sand and drains water faster. Sandy soil does not stay muddy and wet, so your plant's soil will have the opportunity to dry out fast. Repeat this cycle and you will perfect your watering routine.

## DESIGN MIXOLOGY

*Sansevieria cylindrica* looks great in a mix with other plants in a mini garden collection, and they offer contrast to round succulents when planted among them. Their vertical growth allows them to easily share space with other plants without crowding. If planted in an open terrarium, they make a good backdrop for the landscape in glass. Try building a sand garden including *S. cylindrica*. Plant all the plants with soil, then bury them in decorative sand.

OPPOSITE: I love the sword-like spears of *Sansevieria cylindrica*, a variety of the snake plant. It truly is the new modern snake plant.

#ELEPHANTEARPLANT

# *ALOCASIA* AND *COLOCASIA* (ELEPHANT EAR PLANT)

When I see the arrowhead-shaped leaves and strong white veins of *Alocasia amazonica*, I picture the Amazon Jungle filled with giant leaves towering over my head. Exceptional *Alocasia* is dynamic with strong, stiff stems holding heavy, thick leaves. *A. calidora* has tall, upright stems with green leaves but resembles elephant ears. It's just a masterful plant with easy-care needs if you supply the water.

*Colocasia* also are called elephant ears, or taro. There are many varieties; some grow smaller, and some have dark-purple leaves. *Colocasia* Purple Passion or Black Magic varieties have enormous purple leaves that you may see planted in urns outside in the summer sun. Indoors, they pose a challenge to provide enough sunlight and to keep well watered. I say they're well worth the effort if you have the space to keep them. *C. esculenta* Diamond Head love wet feet and are used in water gardens.

## LIGHT

This plant needs a good, bright light source. My *Alocasia amazonica* lives in an eastern window, where morning light hits it daily. Remember that even in the Amazon Jungle, plants like *A. amazonica* living on the forest floor receive only dappled light through the canopy of tropical trees. At certain times of the year, when the sun won't burn the leaves (so, not summer), place them near a sunny window and they will grow more giant leaves.

## WATER

Here is where you must be diligent. The stiff stems of the *Alocasia* are straight upright because they drink up the water like a straw and remain unbent. When an *Alocasia* wilts or the heavy leaves seem to be pulling the stems down, it is because the water supply in the stems is diminishing. Don't be afraid to give this beauty a good pouring of water. Try two pours and then drain out. I often add an extra glass of water between my regular waterings, because I want the plant to drink as much as possible to hold up those stems. This plant enjoys wet soil.

OPPOSITE: *Colocasia*, or elephant ear plant.

Place your *Alocasia* where you can get a good look down at its beautifully veined leaves.

## DESIGN MIXOLOGY

*Alocasia* will enhance any area, especially if you can peer down at those impressive leaves. An area on the floor or on a low table will do it justice, particularly if it's surrounded by shorter plants to increase humidity as well as the jungle look. *Colocasia* will totally jungle up your room. Even as a single specimen, this plant will certainly earn a noticeable gasp of breath from its viewers.

# *TILLANDSIA* (AIR PLANT)

We love our air plants! These unbelievable *Tillandsia* have many shapes, sizes, and colors. You will want to hang and display your air plants all over and anywhere and then change your mind daily. *T. cyanea* 'Anita' has a paddle-shaped spike bract rising from the center of thin slices of green. *Tillandsia* are related to Bromeliads, which are both epiphytes. Epiphytes are plants that take up residence on tropical trees high in the canopies, where they take advantage of more sunlight, tropical breezes, and rainwater. That's how they got their common name—living in the air. *Tillandsia* have specialized leaves with trichomes that give them a silvery white appearance. Trichomes help them catch and absorb water in the crevices of their branches. Evolutionary smarts make them easy-care plants because you should not plant them in soil nor sit them in even the smallest puddle of water, or else they will certainly rot.

## LIGHT

Here is where I go against most written recommendations for air plants, and I speak from my own air plant care testing. Most people suggest indirect light for air plants. Personally, I grow my air plants on a windowsill in a sunny, western exposure in

New York. Of course, the setting sun on the eastern seaboard is quite different from the beating-hot Southwest sun or the rainy, cloudy days of the Pacific Northwest. Even during summer when the setting sun is hot until 9:00 p.m., my air plants are happy and have grown three times their size because I supplement them with adequate shots of water from a plant mister.

## WATER

There are several tricks to watering air plants. *Tillandsia* do need water; they do not live simply on air alone, and our dry indoor environments can sap all moisture away from them. Air plants living in glass globes get shots of wet, misty sprays from my plant mister approximately twice per week. I give them five to eight sprays each time. The air plants either sit on sand or gravel in their glass globes, which help keep excess water away from the plants as it drains into the medium below. My loose air plants get a deep bath once a week. I toss them in a bowl of water and sometimes I forget them overnight. The key here is to shake off excess water after you pull them out of the bath, then you must sit them on something that will absorb the excess water that drips off their bodies. I use a microfiber pad that would otherwise be used to sit your washed dishes on to drip dry. Make sure these precious creatures do not sit in dripping water, or they will rot.

## DESIGN MIXOLOGY

Once you have the basic care down, then air plants are a no-brainer. Air plants can be tucked into a flower arrangement or sit on a windowsill with your favorite objects. Perfect design mixology specimens!

I make hanging glass globes for all occasions. I like to change my living displays for holidays and create seasonal scenes inside the glass domes. I add air plants and change the scene in summer with seashells from the beach or create a snapshot of nature with a mini plastic figurine owl peering out at me. When you hang multiple globes, use odd numbers, such as three hanging at varied levels, so your eye bounces from one to another. You can sit flat-bottomed glass globes on a coffee table, your nightstand, or use multiples as an interesting centerpiece. You can mix and match your table decor for an inspiring table setting. If you put a fabric runner down the center of the table, sit several *Tillandsia*-filled globes down the middle, then add glass globes holding lit votive candles. Candlelight always creates a magical setting.

OPPOSITE: Air plants can sit anywhere, even on wire hangers in mid-air. Here in the bathroom their trichomes can drink in the warm, humid air from your shower.

# *HAWORTHIA* (ZEBRA CACTUS)

*Haworthia* is the regal specimen of the succulent world. This strong plant gives us many reasons to think it stately. I visualize its stiff upward growth as the spikes of a crown. These spikes with their attractive white lines stay this way year-round. They are so sweet to glance upon on any surface with a light source. When *Haworthia* is planted with other succulents, it always breaks up the design pleasantly and pulls your focus toward its white stripes.

## LIGHT

*Haworthia* does not require as much light as the leafy *Echeveria* or *Crassula* jade plant. Succulents in general love sunlight, but *Haworthia* is a bit more forgiving and tolerant of lower or indirect light levels. If you sit these plants under a grow light, they will survive for a while but may grow leggy over time. Natural light is the best source.

BELOW: Nestling inside a gold-accented terrarium is the kind of royal treatment *Haworthia* deserves.

OPPOSITE: Queen *Haworthia* looking regal in her spotted crown.

## WATER

*Haworthia* spreads its tolerance levels to a watering threshold too. You can stretch out the watering cycle a bit longer than other succulents—but don't forget it. If you see brown on the crown's tips, then your *Haworthia* has gone past the threshold and needs watering. Give the plant one or two ounces of water and adequate drainage. Find the sweet spot of moisture needs and your plant will live a long and healthy reign.

## DESIGN MIXOLOGY

*Haworthia* can live in many planting scenarios. Its upward crown was made to form-fit geometric terrariums, and gold accents elevate the design to make it look rich. You use the dome terrarium on bookshelves if there is a light source nearby. This terrarium could be lovely in a bathroom by scented candlelight or with matching soap canisters. The terrarium has one open segment that provides the opportunity for humidity to evaporate out.

# PLANTS, CATS, AND DOGS

We love our pets; they are part of our families. We care for them like family, especially when it comes to their health and welfare. The love for a cat or a dog that lives with us for ten, fifteen, or twenty years is very real.

As we love our pets, we want them to coexist with our increasing love for our houseplant jungle. One of the many things you can do as a pet caretaker is know the behavior of your pet. Is your pet a nibbler, digger, or climber?

## WARNING

The suggestions you read here are only suggestions. You must do your own research, consult with your veterinarian, and watch your pets closely to make sure you do all you can to keep them safe and protect them from harm.

The ASPCA website (www.aspca.org/pet-care/animal-poison-control/toxic-and-non-toxic-plants) has an extensive, alphabetical list of plants that are toxic and nontoxic to dogs and cats. For example, *Monstera deliciosa* is toxic to dogs and cats, and *Calathea* is not recommended for human or animal consumption.

No animals or plants were harmed in the taking of this book's photographs.

## NIBBLER

Let me introduce you to our feline models Brooklyn, a calico female, and Mac, a fluffy golden male. Brooklyn and Mac live happy lives in Williamsburg, Brooklyn, with their Instagram mom, Meagan Rosson. Mac and Brooklyn are helping exhibit how we as pet owners can create safe environments for our pets.

Cats enjoy plants. They can hide behind them. They can sit in the soil inside the pot, if it is large enough. Then they can jump out and track soil all over. Now, that doesn't sound good.

My cat, Smudgie, is not a jumper or climber—and I am lucky. We have become so close; we speak to each other in a language we both comprehend. I may not meow, but my eyes and my tone of voice convey the messages that keep her in line.

If I simply put the plants off the floor and onto shelves and tables, she really could care less about them. I have a spider plant (*Chlorophytum comosum*) with dangling spider babies that I allowed to hang too low and within range of occasional whops from Smudgie's paw. As a conscientious cat owner and plant lover, I thought it in the best interest of all involved to move the spider plant higher and out of her reach. This way, the plant babies wouldn't be torn off the plant, and Smudgie wouldn't be able to put them in her mouth.

Mac seems to be the nibbler in this family as he tries to sneak a nip on the *Calathea lancifolia*.

## DIGGER

If your cat or dog loves to dig in soil, you might struggle with keeping larger pots on the floor. You could try putting a bit of wire grid on the topsoil to deter paws. Or try placing plastic film on the lid of the pot, but not on the soil, then poke some holes to allow moisture to evaporate. Dogs are less likely to try to dig in a planted pot if they can't get to it because of the furniture surrounding the pot. Your cat might be more determined to jump over objects and furniture to sit in your potted plant and hide.

## CLIMBER

Meagan Rosson has installed wall climbing devices to give her cats the opportunity to climb. This is also the cats' space. If it works, the cats may stay away from the plants because they have their own areas to jump, climb, and play as it naturally comes to them.

As we add more houseplants to our collections, we need to educate ourselves on which ones might be toxic to our beloved pets. Most times, the issue is gastrointestinal and your pet will simply vomit. Some plants are poisonous to humans as well as to pets, and you may want to stay away from keeping those in your menagerie.

## NON-PET-FRIENDLY PLANTS

Plants in the genus *Euphorbia* leak a white sap when their stems break or become damaged. This sap can drip down to the floor. If your pets lick it, it might swell their tongues and make them sick. *Euphorbia* includes many wonderful specimens. If you grow these plants, find a way to protect your furry loved ones from ingesting or chewing on the leaves, branches, or licking the sap.

Here are a few common *Euphorbia* species to own with caution around your pets:

- **Poinsettia (*Euphorbia pulcherrima*)**: This plant has red bracts and is grown for the Christmas holiday season.
- **Pencil Cactus (*Euphorbia tirucalli*)**: A long, upward-branching succulent.
- **Crown of Thorns (*Euphorbia milii*)**: This plant looks very biblical with its thick thorny stems; the flowers are also bracts of pink, red, white, or yellow.

OPPOSITE: Meagan Rosson (on Instagram as @plant_lady_is_the_new_cat_lady) keeps plants on higher shelves. The shelves themselves are not easy to leap onto, which keeps Mac and Brooklyn from nibbling freely. As you see, Mac is still trying to cultivate a method of climbing within reach of their collection of plants.

# II.

# INDOOR GARDENING STYLE

**THE URBAN JUNGLE TREND** has created a huge curiosity for giant tropical houseplants. Containers that hold our desired plants can be installed on walls, hung from ceiling hooks, and attached to shelves. One of my favorite objects to repurpose is a short ladder. Imagine green plants sitting on ladder rungs with their vines spilling down.

Bringing plants indoors doesn't stop with containers, though. You can include in your decorations leaf-patterned fabrics and tropical wallpaper, or even coasters and placemats with a *Monstera* leaf pattern. Small lapel pins in the shape of *Monstera* leaves, cacti, or succulents can be purchased on several Etsy sites. One clever creator is Samantha Leung, who runs the shop Hemleva. Find more in Section III.

Vintage card catalog with English ivy's (*Hedera helix*) long, trailing vines that seem to have their own vintage vibe.

Indoor gardening has evolved to include so many interior design visions. Design themes such as urban jungle, botanical styling, bohemian or boho, and industrial chic have proven to be the latest and most sought-after looks to bring to our interior spaces.

**Botanical styling** interior design is an interpretation of all things, well, botanical. This trend includes walls covered with botanical prints, herbarium specimens, and vintage garden prints; antique signage or seed packets; and porcelain teacups filled with mini plants or violets.

My interpretation of **boho** is bright, mixed colors, such as orange, pink, and yellow, with lots of pillows on the bed or couch. You might use big, repeating prints of wallpaper in a giddy dream with multiple fabric combinations to fill a room with rich color. Find the plants to complement and continue the scheme.

**Industrial** pieces can mix nicely into various interior styles. You can use a large stainless-steel Metro shelving unit on wheels for your potted plants and collectibles

Carefully placed green foliage and soft pillows on which to rest your head in a room full of blue, a soothing hue, as houseplants act as organic air purifiers, make this a place to dream.

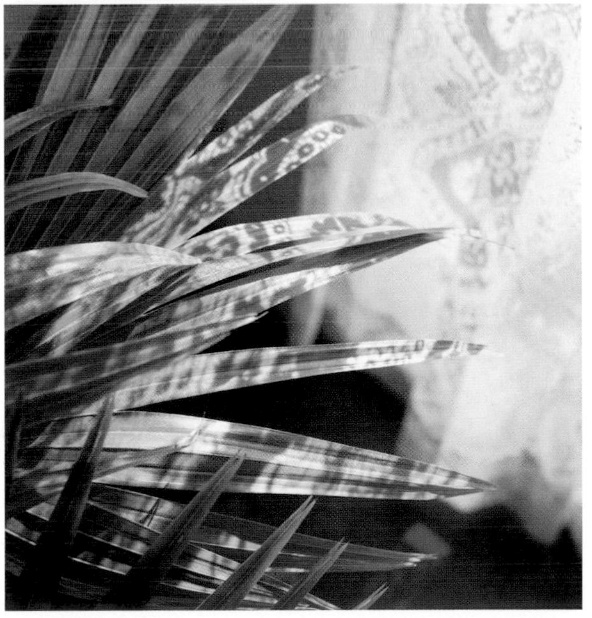

TOP LEFT: This metal cabinet is one of my favorite flea market finds. I discovered it on a summer day I spent walking around in the Queens neighborhood of Long Island City, home of the famous East River waterfront Pepsi sign. It shows off my most precious plant specimens and keep them protected.

ABOVE: I love this room. Here you can read intellectual musings or books on famous periods of art, or just take a nap in the setting sun and not think at all.

LEFT: Summer sun gently bathes this Chinese fan palm. These are the days when you open the windows and let the curtains wave in the warm breezes. You and your plants sit feeling content and relaxed while the warmth of the sun hits you.

Hanging planters fill our vertical space, so we can have room for indoor plants in abundance. Planters that were traditionally used in outdoor gardening are now being utilized in new and distinctive ways, such as this foliage chandelier.

that moves around the room with the sunlight for a seasonal change. Industrial design looks like it sounds: old metal, peeling paint chips, and brick warehouse space all come to mind. Search for an aged metal single-rod clothes rack that you can dangle moss-ball kokedama plants with hanging philodendron tendrils and lime-colored *Pothos* leaves for a movable feast of chartreuse. Pick one piece and incorporate it into your room to accommodate your newest plant collection.

Why not include the term **retro**? This can refer to chairs, tables, refrigerators, and color schemes that mimic and represent decor of the 1950s. Smeg refrigerators are so great looking combined with chrome-legged tables and chairs, turning your kitchen into your own personal diner. How fun to find retro planters that will look great with mint green kitchen appliances!

This list of design themes would be incomplete without my favorite: **kitsch**. The description for kitsch runs the gamut of art, objects, or design from sentimental to tacky, but with appreciation for its ironic and humorous look. The word *kitsch* refers to a time in 1800s Germany when inexpensive art was popular and marketable.

For me, kitsch exists in a place of sweet 1950s collector planters and old furniture with fabric that recalls summer bungalows at the beach when I was a kid and lifelong memories were made. The collection might not be glamorous, but the look makes me crack a laugh or smile with the emotions and memories it brings.

# PLANTERS OF INTEREST

Planters elevate outstanding houseplants. Planters complement interior design and decor and can be specially chosen to show off a style. You can choose a pot for a specific plant because of the plant's growth pattern. I mention growth pattern because some plants have an architectural or sculptural element to them. Why not utilize the plant's shape and search for a fashionable pot to purchase that adds additional interest? Each of us has a love for a certain material, whether it is terra cotta, ceramic, wood, basket weaves, metal, or the newest material trend, cement. We can apply the right plant to the right planter.

## MID-CENTURY CERAMICS

The design of the room on page 60 gives me a feel from the past; maybe you can call it old fashioned. It was fun picking plants that would suit these 1950s ceramic planters. I took a random collection of ferns, snake plants, succulents, and scraggly, pale ivy, which completes the kitsch feel.

The chair became my focal point and I played around with the floor plants such as the fiddle-leaf fig and *Monstera* to see how they fit with the furniture. Would I be able to walk around the plants and not damage them if I brushed my leg on the leaves? Would I enjoy having the plants next to the chair to view while having my morning coffee or reading a book on houseplants? Asking yourself questions on how you will use the room will assist you in finding where to place the bigger plants.

Why is growth pattern important when choosing a planter? Ferns and ivy tend to spill over the edge of a pot, thus hiding the rim. *Alocasia*'s tall, stiff stems expose the pot—this style of growth begs you pick a planter to show off both plant and pot. *Colocasia* have a Victorian or Old World image to them. If you pot up your specimen houseplant in period finds, you may just be transported to another time and place.

### LIGHT

A wide selection of plants can be considered here because the ample sunlight supplies the environment for the plants to thrive. The design decisions are easy with plenty of light streaming in from the doorway and the windows. Almost anywhere in the room is an appropriate place for houseplants.

## HOYA

*Hoya* are somewhere between foliage and succulent plants. They have thick, leathery leaves and withstand neglect and abuse. I started my small *Hoya* gem from two leaves with root cuttings. Months later, it had a 6-inch-long tendril. It lives in a 3-inch pot, yet I feel so impressed with its growth progress.

**LIGHT:** *Hoya* like hot indoor sun. Mine sits on a western-lit windowsill.

**WATER:** I let the soil go dry and then I pour a few ounces of water to drain through and out of the pot.

**DESIGN MIXOLOGY:** As the vines of *Hoya* grow longer they look handsome as hanging plants near a light-filled window or sitting on a shelf with strands falling over the ledge. My *Hoya* is a small specimen that lives on the kitchen windowsill in a design mixology of air plants in glass globes amongst more 3-inch terra cotta pots planted with succulents.

ABOVE: I was inspired by my green Hull and McCoy 1950s planters to add a *Monstera* leaf pattern fabric runner, a final complement to the vignette. I found this vintage green pot on my aunt's back porch; she'd long forgotten it was there under a pile of broken terra cotta pots and decaying maple leaves. Imagine my surprise to discover this planter is from the 1950s, a mid-century McCoy basketweave design made in the United States.

OPPOSITE: A trio of green planters with the indestructible ZZ plant (*Zamioculcas zamiifolia*). Hull pottery (the lower right pot) was made in Crooksville, Ohio, starting in 1905 by Addis E. Hull, who later bought the Acme Pottery Company. The gloss artwares of the 1950s were a popular, new style back then.

## DESIGN MIXOLOGY

The bookshelf became a genuine collection of craft projects and vintage collectibles. All these elements tell the story about this room inspired from objects of the past and the comfort their memories bring. You may have to buy yourself a set of *Monstera melamine* plates to complete the breakfast nook you just designed. The modern-day incarnation of the past with present-day home decor is fun to incorporate into the design.

In my design mixology, I like to create expressive vignettes that speak to a certain snapshot of life. Some days, I am a scavenger picking through the artifacts of my family's discarded decor. I am big on finding inspiration from vintage anything. Period ceramic planters full of greenery create living decor that reminds us of an idea, activity, or feeling from another age. I like decor artifacts from a past time with a distinctive look. It is a bit like fashion or art, which evolves within a decade to represent the culture of the time. How does an era fit into your life?

## MID-CENTURY POTS WITH STANDS

Pots with attractive wooden stands become instant decor. You can plunk them wherever they match your decor, and they look terrific sitting on the floor. These particular pots (see one on page 65) with stands become an additional piece of furniture in your space. Most of the industry has labeled them "mid-century modern." Think of Don Draper's stylish office in *Mad Men*, the acclaimed TV series about Madison Avenue advertising firms in 1960s New York City where the convention of cocktails at lunch was fashionable.

In 2012, while I ventured to create my own workshop lectures, I noticed a startup business in New York City called the Sill, which was delivering plants to local offices and doorsteps. The founder, Eliza Blank, used this style of pot at the very onset.

## ZZ PLANT

*Zamioculcas zamiifolia* is a tongue-twister of a name, so most people call it ZZ plant. This plant is so sturdy and easy to care for that it belongs in everyone's collection. ZZ's smooth, shiny, and verdant leaves should receive just the right amount of light. When you locate that sweet spot of light, then new, long multi-leaved stems will pop up weekly.

**LIGHT:** ZZ is known for tolerating low light, so too much intense sun will burn the tender, petal-like leaves.
**WATER:** Do not drown your ZZ plant or keep its soil soggy. A moderate watering will do and then let the soil dry to the touch. Remember, a ZZ plant's water intake is affected by seasons, so cut back in winter.
**DESIGN MIXOLOGY:** ZZ plant's stems grow upward and hold themselves stiffly so you can surround its pot with other plants, artifacts, and books. The plant will be seen above the rest.

It was smart looking and fit with most decor, an instant potted plant in your office or home. It seems so simple, but many great ideas are just that—fresh and simple. Her company motto: Plants make people happy.

Later, in 2017, two West Coast guys named Nicolas Bartoli and Ron Radu joined the plant delivery business with their company Leon & George, based in San Francisco and Los Angeles, California. Leon & George also uses its own style of the mid-century wooden stand planter.

### DESIGN MIXOLOGY

I had to own this West Elm set (see opposite page). This particular style is described as a planter "inspired by the clean silhouettes of the '50s and '60s" and West Elm calls

I couldn't resist having my very own mid-century-style pot with a wood stand. It is so stylish. The white pot will easily mix with decor, furniture, and painted walls of all colors.

them "turned-leg standing planters." The wood legs and ceramic pot inspired me to go with a clean, white, assorted display on top of a white wood shelving unit tucked into the corner under the slanted white ceiling. This gardening story evolved like a puzzle as I fit all the pieces together.

White can be interpreted as clean and pure. I see the color white as fresh alongside green living, the contrast to dark, rich soil. Green can be interpreted as a regenerative hue; I included the plump *Aloe vera* with its healing gel to bring it together even further. The DIG poster reminds me that it's all about rich soil and the love of getting my hands grubby. I must confess the cat plate reminded me of my own cat, Smudgie, and I made it the focal point of the display. The eye zooms in on the black outline of the illustrated

ABOVE: Mid-century modern wood furniture and gold accent lighting add warmth to spread of plants in this gray room.

BELOW: These decadent gold succulent planters come courtesy of Amelie Sebastian of My Little Greens, and pair well with the marble-topped coffee table and some good reading for a cozy mid-century vibe.

plate and from there begins to read the other objects in the display. It all fits. This design mixology snapshot fits my memories and my own life. I share them with you as examples of how you can create your own design storyline.

Here, my love of digging in the dirt speaks from the poster. The white ceramic pots elevate the plants. This white corner lent itself to a motif where delicate fern fronds unfurl out of the deep well of the pot. The nearby stiff, juicy aloe points you to the illustration, which shows a bit of whimsy. Just like the room with the green-leaved pillows and comfy chair on page 60, it has its own private corner.

Mid-century influence rises from the past to find design residence in our green jungle. Maybe you have an assortment of collectibles in the closet and can reinvent or purpose them for your plants. It's time to go on a hunt to find the perfect planter from a time long, long ago.

## ALOE VERA

*Aloe vera* is made of soft, sap-filled succulent spikes and is a life-giving, life-affirming green plant. I am quite fond of the *Aloe vera* plant because of how it feels to the touch. I like to run my fingers along the smooth spikes of green that jut up, pointing skyward. This species exists in a dry landscape as if the gods put it there to protect us humans with its healing powers from the burning hot sun.

**LIGHT:** *Aloe vera* are succulents and need good sunlight to flourish. Do your best to provide light and your plant will grow new branches with a plump bulk faster. New growth comes from the base at the center, ever pointing upward. This species has a slight white dot pattern on its skin.

**WATER:** Most succulents like a good, full drink of water that drains through the soil. Then you let it dry out to breathe before adding water again. I do not like to let my succulents dry to the point where their leaves turn brown, shrivel up, and fall off. If too many leaves die off, the plant starts to lose its structure. I may water my succulents more than most, but I do make sure they receive the sunlight that will help them use up that extra water supply. I prefer to leave the drought in the desert lands.

**DESIGN MIXOLOGY:** *Aloe vera*'s spiky upward leaf growth lends itself to slender designs without branching out sideways. This gives you the opportunity to slip the plant in among objects or other plants in a tight spot. The planter can sit behind a picture frame with the leaf spikes popping up as a backdrop. Those leaf spikes hold their position in your story display and do not lean on other plants—a good, strong choice for a leafy snapshot.

## FLEA MARKET FINDS

Flea-market shopping can become addictive. You meander up and down the aisles of vendor booths filled with an infinite array of collectibles, furniture, and items you would never have imagined you can fill with plants—but you will imagine it at the flea market. Find the location for a fabulous event near your area.

In New Milford, Connecticut, is an admired flea market called the Elephant's Trunk. It's a favorite spot featured on *Flea Market Flip*. This enormous market was founded in 1976 as a country market and has since become a phenomenal event. People drive for miles in the early morning hours and wait in line to begin their treasure hunts.

## *CYRTOMIUM FALCATUM* (HOLLY FERN)

Holly ferns are a bit different from other ferns because they need less humidity. They have a leathery leaf that is less delicate to breakage or browning up from dry air. They also have a more defined look—I like how the stems reach out from the center with each pointy petal off the center stem.

**LIGHT:** Indirect light is the preference of most ferns, and holly ferns are no different. But if you have a bright window with a bit of morning sun, this fern can take it.

**WATER:** The key to holly ferns is keeping their soil evenly moist. When holly fern fronds feel deprived of moisture, they will turn yellow immediately, giving you the opportunity to assess their needs. Do you have the plant in the right place for light, or do you need to alter your watering schedule? You can even take this little wonder to the sink and run some lukewarm water over its leaflets. It will reward you with shiny fronds.

**DESIGN MIXOLOGY:** Holly ferns have a strong look and widely fan out. Sit the plants in an area where you can view their interesting growth. I chose to put mine on the bottom shelf of this étagère so it can be viewed from above. It almost fills the entire shelf.

Often, I pick something up that was thrown out on the side of the road; I call it roadside antique shopping. One person's trash is another person's treasure. My husband teases me that my perfect price tag is $5 or free! There it was, waiting for me on the sidewalk, discarded without thought—my perfect folding plant stand. I decided not to repaint it because I like the aging rust.

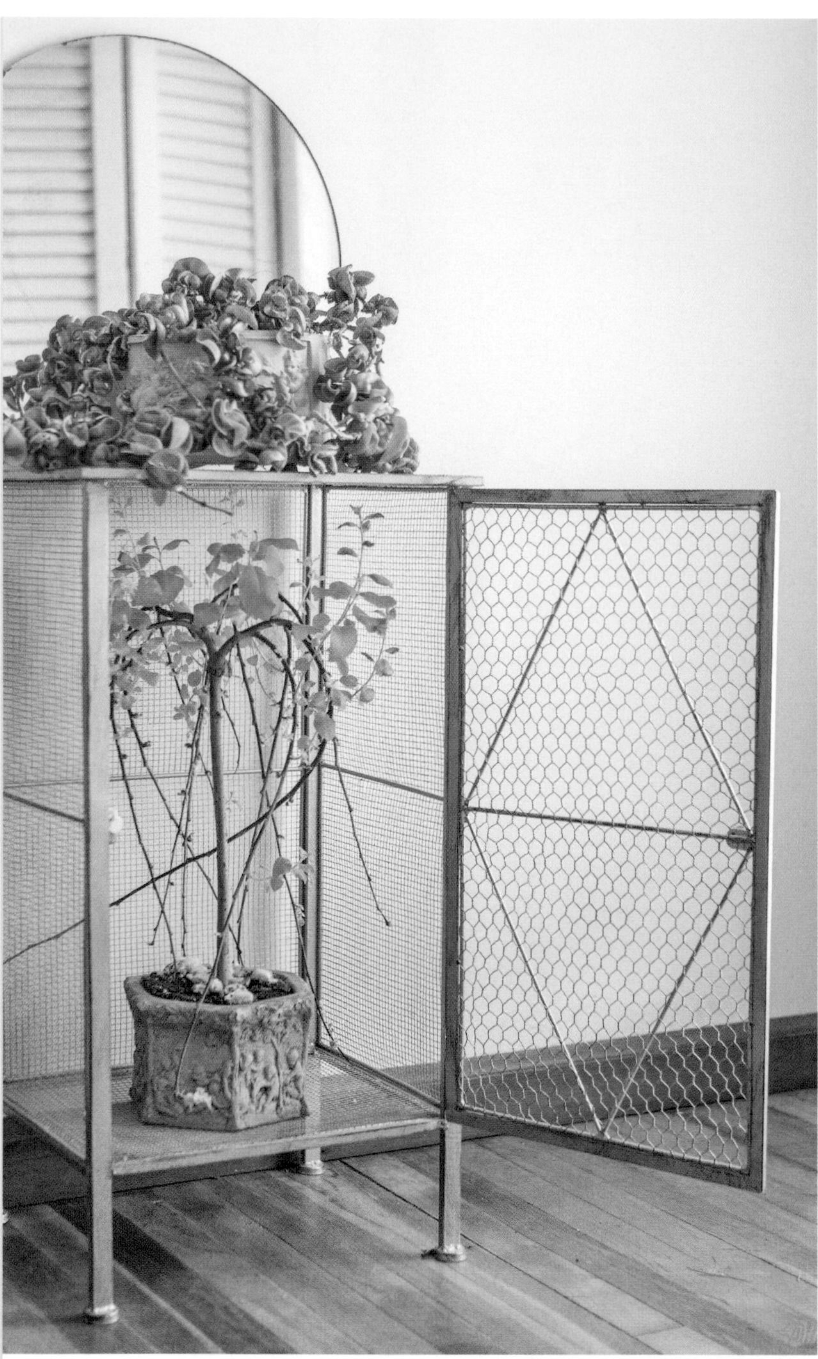

How pleasing this wire cabinet becomes when you open the door to view your living treasure.

One summer day, I drove up to the Elephant's Trunk to find enough fun stuff to fill a football field. The trip was well worth it, even if I only went home with a $5 mid-century lamp that I absolutely love. It has the most perfect round, aqua shade to match the exact color of my bedroom walls.

One of the vendors had a sugar mold commonly used in Colonial times—a long, rectangular piece of wood with small, round indentations that seem perfect for deviled eggs. I kicked myself for not buying the sugar mold; I wanted to plant it with succulents. Google the item, or look it up on Pinterest, or maybe someone on Etsy has them available. At flea markets, you can find whatever you might fancy to house your increasing collection of living plants. Happy treasure hunting!

## PLANTERS OF WHIMSY

As serious as I can be about design and matching the right plant to the right pot, I am serious about delightful, amusing planters like the one below. I call them planters of whimsy. Whimsy puts a smile on my face, lightens my daily burdens, and brings on the cute factor—it has its proper place, a gratifying pop of endearing charm.

## MODERN ARTISAN PLANTER

Concrete? Yes, it seems like an unlikely material to make lovely handmade artisan planters with. But that's exactly the popular interest for small planters, particularly sitting in multiples filled to the brim with succulents. I see this style of planter fitting well alongside rustic furniture, a modern marble kitchen counter, or mixed with bath and body products on a shelf in your bathroom.

Plants feel seasonal changes in sunlight no matter where they live. So, as we care for our plant collections in concrete, we must take these environmental constraints into our care plan. Learn more about light considerations for your succulents on page 19.

ABOVE: A collector's fancy of vintage cans, such as Hunt's tomato paste filled with *Haworthia*. These classic designs are charming planters sitting on a kitchen windowsill with lots of hot sun for cacti and succulents.

BELOW: Another West Elm purchase, my white ceramic turtle planter appears to be walking on the ledge, carrying a load of succulents. Mr. Turtle had to come home with me because I knew he would fit perfectly on this glass shelf stuffed with *Echeveria* and *Crassula* jade plants.

ABOVE: Succulents are tolerant of drying soil and cramped growing places, but one thing they really do not live well without is light. Here are my favorite plants—*Cryptanthus* and *Echeveria* galore—bathing in the sun in my marvelous MadPotters collection.

RIGHT: See how quickly the pots become sculptures when green succulents are added. Small cement pots are adorable to line up in a row and fill with a selection of succulents with different growth patterns.

## CRYPTANTHUS

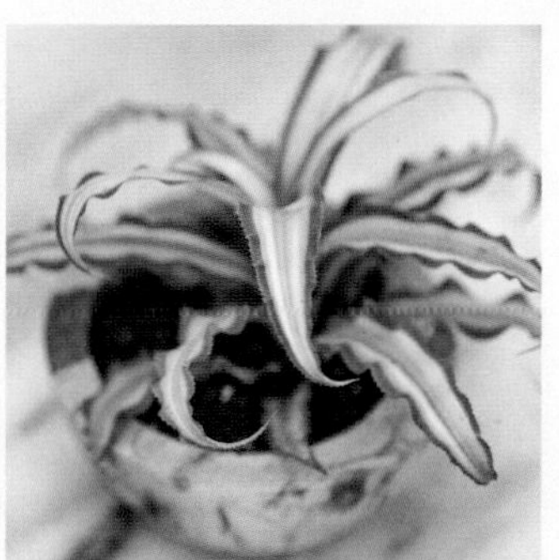

*Cryptanthus* is a favorite plant of mine, because it holds up in terrariums for years. Its leaves arch out from its center with stripes of green.

**LIGHT:** This plant can handle bright sunlight, but not all day. Its coloring will deepen with more sun.
**WATER:** Give it a deep drink of water and then let the top of the soil dry a bit until its next drench. If the tips turn brown, it has become too dry.
**DESIGN MIXOLOGY:** Use pots that will enhance the plant's arching leaf pattern by letting it spill over the edge a bit, then place it where you can easily view those arches and get an aerial view of their stripes.

### MATERIAL

MadPotters's Christie Lothrop took me though a little tutorial to understand the craft behind the pot. She uses Cement All, as she explains that concrete has sand and rocks added to it, but Cement All can be a much quicker alternative to sifting out the rocks by hand. Then Christie uses powdered color made specifically for cement to create the blacks, grays, and colored pieces, because the cement does not come pre-colored. For the paint accents, she uses spray paint and painter's tape—never stencils.

MadPotters uses recycled plastic for most everything, including storing and mixing, which limits the number of pieces that can be made before the mold breaks. All pots and colors are hand-mixed by Christie, making this crafter's collection one of a kind.

### MOLDS & CREATING SHAPES

For molds, excluding the shooters, MadPotters does not use silicone or pre-made molds. Her pots are unique because she uses found items for molds, basically anything plastic that catches her eye, such as Chinese soup to-go containers and plastic water pitchers. The most challenging part is finding two random pieces that will fit together to make a nice-sized indentation for planting. The result makes the rim of every bowl unique.

ABOVE: A collection of Christie Lothrop's marble- and copper-accented pots and trays.

OPPOSITE: These pots of varying shapes but matching designs are perfect complements of each other.

## TIPS FOR WATERING SUCCULENTS

Succulents are drought-hearty plants and need well-draining soil; they are easily susceptible to stem rot. Make sure the entire pot is dry before your next watering, and always make sure to give it a good soak through each time. The key is to dry them through to the bottom of the pot. When it comes time to water again, you will be sure to see the water drain right through and out the bottom drain hole. For those in-between spots, a small squeeze bottle with a long spout really helps keep water off the leaves. Place your succulents in a bright location with plenty of direct sunlight to keep them happy!

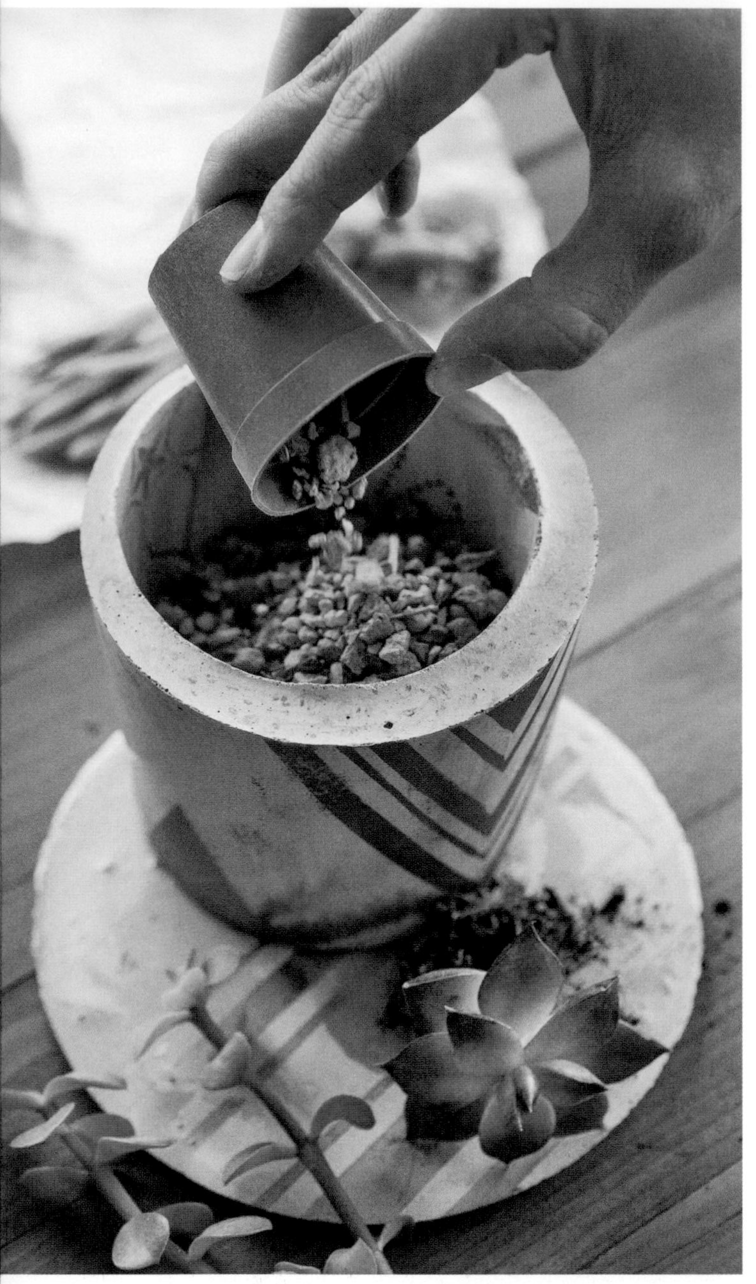

### HOW TO PLANT SUCCULENTS

- Many indoor gardeners use succulent cuttings purchased from suppliers. You can also make your own by buying small, 1- to 2-inch pots of succulents, and then cut the stem away from the pot right above the roots. Leave the cutting out for a day or two until the cut hardens and heals, and then the cutting is ready to plant.

- Now you are ready to lay out your materials. You should have a bag of small gravel, your pots, and enough succulent cuttings or plants to fill the pots. One planting style is to pack succulents in tightly against each other.

- After you match your plants and pots together, fill your pot halfway with gravel. Arrange the plants in a sweet design. Top off the design to the edge of the container with the rest of the gravel. Magical!

## DESIGN MIXOLOGY

Succulents in all their wonderfulness come in shades of green or greenish-blues, some with leaves edged with red or pink. You may want to mix or keep to one color combination, or you may choose purity in collecting and use only one style or pattern. I tend to lean this way because many pots clumped together pulls off a grander display and visually offers a "wow" impact. Others may choose to have a singular specimen sitting on a counter or table, showing off its serious importance.

As you pull your cuttings together into larger containers, think about how you will view your potted succulents. From above, facing forward on a shelf, or on a windowsill? This will guide you in arranging the plants. Taller succulents, such as blue-ish *Senecio*, will stand behind the small suction-cup leaves of *Crassula ovata* 'Gollum' jade.

The perfect spot for the perfect plant in the perfect pot.

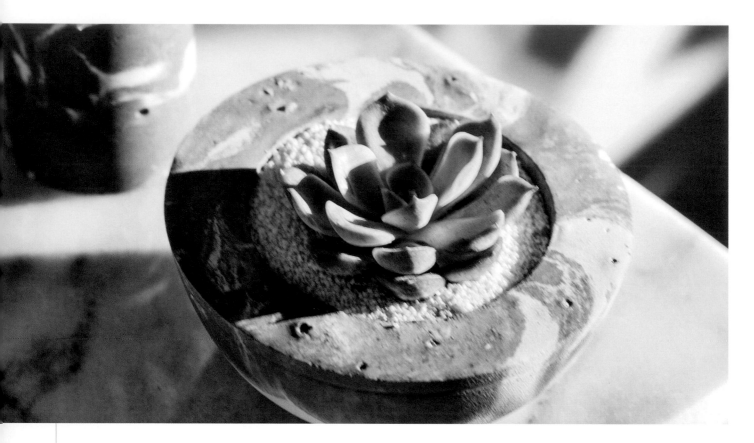

ABOVE: A sweet *Echeveria* planted in crystal sand in a darling cement pot. One impressive plant in your favorite pot looks special, growing with a marvelous beauty.

BELOW: *Echeveria* is the king of all succulents and comes in dozens of varieties, colors, and leafy rosettes too countless to track.

Contemporary breeders give their varieties clever nicknames. Use a large, curly *Echeveria* 'Lace' or 'Curly Locks'. *Echeveria gibbiflora* has pink leaf edges and resembles kale. Also try *Echeveria runyonii* 'Topsy Turvy', a much lighter pale green with leaves that turn inward at the end. As you gaze down into the center of its rosette, a deep, small, and tightly wound center, you see life unfolding before you.

## HANGING WIRE CHANDELIER

The term "chandelier" has become this planter's buzzword because it can be hung above from the ceiling, a tree, an awning, a porch, or a terrace. On the next page, I'll show you how to make one.

Hanging wire plant holders can be incarnated into different otherworldly styles in infinite possibilities. You can hang them over your dining table as an entertainment display. Floral arrangement trends include juicy *Echeveria* and various succulents integrated with foliage. If you combine foliage plants and flowering orchids, it becomes a dangling centerpiece. Combine a few unusual stems from the florist and you create an exotic arrangement. Try ginger or bird of paradise and heads of *Protea* or *Anthurium*. What a sight of exotic beauty.

If green foliage is your look, think of adding a Staghorn fern or an Elkhorn fern (*Platycerium*). Both have incredible long leaves that mimic caribou racks. They will protrude out of the arrangement and hang down, if you are lucky to find a specimen with long leaf extensions. You can shop the look and purchase supplies at Terrain (see Resources, page 160).

This is indoor gardening. Wire holders have commonly been used in outdoor gardens with annuals for summer color display. Holders are built strong and can hold weight, so they make perfect planters to convert for indoor greenery. You can replant them from season to season or replace plants that might not have survived over time. Depending on your collection of plants, their light requirements will vary. If you choose to create a temporary arrangement, then light is not even an issue.

At my home, I planted mine with soft fronds of maidenhair ferns (*Adiantum*), which need to keep their roots wet. Keeping the soil soggy might be a challenge. Tropical maidenhair ferns grow between mossy, wet rocks near waterfalls in their native environment. You can try using peat moss, which holds moisture, like a wet bog. Always have a spray mister nearby to give them a daily misting of water. It is known in the plant community that the delicate, lovely maidenhair fern can die even on the most diligent indoor gardener—but we continue to try because they are instantly divine.

Behold the versatile wire plant holder. Make it your own with foliage, orchids, and ethereal ferns—or even *Monstera* leaves. Hang it above in full view.

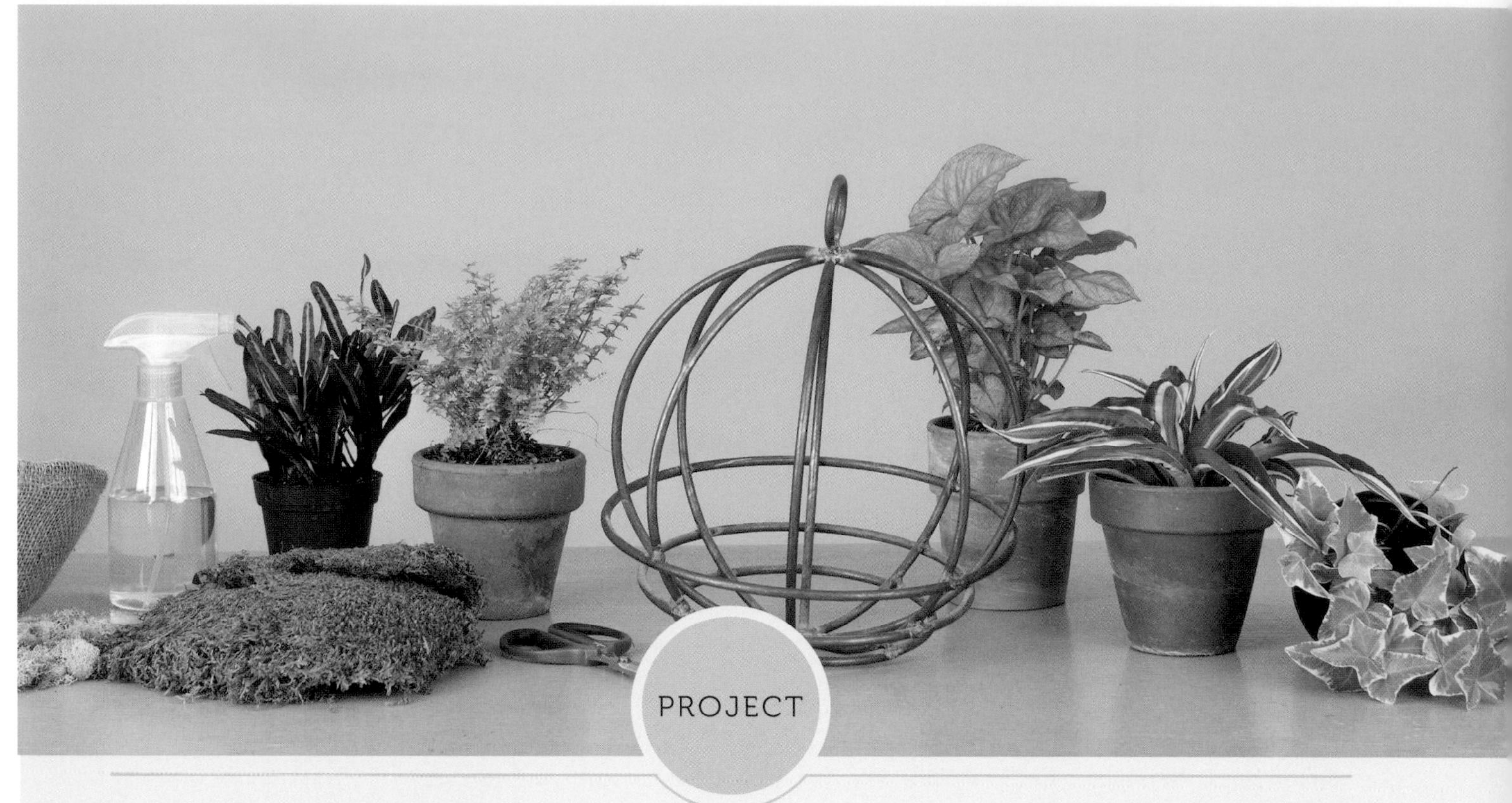


# HANGING WIRE CHANDELIER

## STEP-BY-STEP

Let me show you an easy step-by-step project to create your own chandelier. Before you start to build it, play with the arrangement of plants on a table until you are satisfied with how they look. You may choose the most vibrant of the group to create a focal point that will bring your eye to the center.

### MATERIALS

- Wire holder
- Liner (natural jute, coco fiber)
- Sheet moss (green, dried and preserved)
- Potting soil, houseplant variety
- Water mister
- Scissors
- Loose reindeer moss
- Gardening gloves (optional)

### PLANT SELECTION

- *Dracaena warneckii*
- *Croton*
- *Hedera helix* (English ivy)
- *Nephrolepis exaltata* (ruffle fern)
- *Nephthytis* (arrowhead)

1. After gathering your materials, begin to layer the larger pieces of sheet moss into the wire cage. This will hide the liner and give the arrangement a greener look. Push it up against the wire so as not to leave any spaces.

2. Fold the jute liner so it slides through the wire opening, and then slowly open it in place before you place it onto the moss. This is an important step to be conscientious while doing, because once you add soil and plants, it will be difficult to move. So, make sure it sits securely on the moss and is adequately hidden from view.

3. It is crucial that you place the plants in the exact place you want them to end up at the end of the planting. As you pull your plants out of their pots, you may shake off some of the soil to make the rootball smaller, especially if you cannot fit it through the open space. If there are lots of thick roots, simply snip and prune some off; there are plenty of roots for the plant to survive if you trim off a few. You can also squeeze or compress the rootball with your hands to further reduce its size to fit into the open slot.

4. As you continue to build your arrangement one plant at a time, tilt some of the plants to show them off as your focal point. For example, this *Dracaena warneckii* is positioned so its dynamic white and green stripes are the center of the grouping. First, put the plant into the space and then gently tilt the rootball on its side. Pull gently on the leaves so they are outside the wire cage. It is a bit of a manual challenge. As you see the grouping getting fuller with each additional plant, you will be adding the taller plants centrally in the cage, so they will be seen above the shorter outer foliage.

5. Make sure each plant has been adequately watered before placing it in the wire cage. We do not want to add unnecessary amounts of water. As you add each plant, you can give the soil a shot of moisture with the water mister. Misting further compacts loose soil and ensures the plants have enough water. Then, at completion, you do not have to do any watering for at least a week.

6. The arrangement is beginning to really fill out and look dramatic. Here I am filling in the back of the planter with green foliage to make a full and healthy-looking hanger. The interior of the cage is beginning to get tight and you might find that you have to remove some soil and roots from each individual plant you add so that they all can fit into the cage.

7. If you find that you have empty spots or spaces, you can fill them in with bits of moss here and there. If the moss has gotten stiff, give it a misting to soften the pieces. You really don't have to add any moss if the plants you have chosen cascade over the rim of the insert and sheet moss, hiding any empty spaces there might be.

8. The central *Dracaena* creates a nice visual next to the *Nephthytis*. The colors of the plants mix well and your eye follows around to catch the *Croton* on the left with its thin, multi-colored spears poking up from the group. Your chandelier should stay rather wet longer than potted plants because there is no drainage. You can add water to plants individually if the soil around one is wet and another seems drier. Poke your finger into the soil throughout to get a sense of its moisture level. Then use your mister and shoot streams of water around those plants that need a drink.

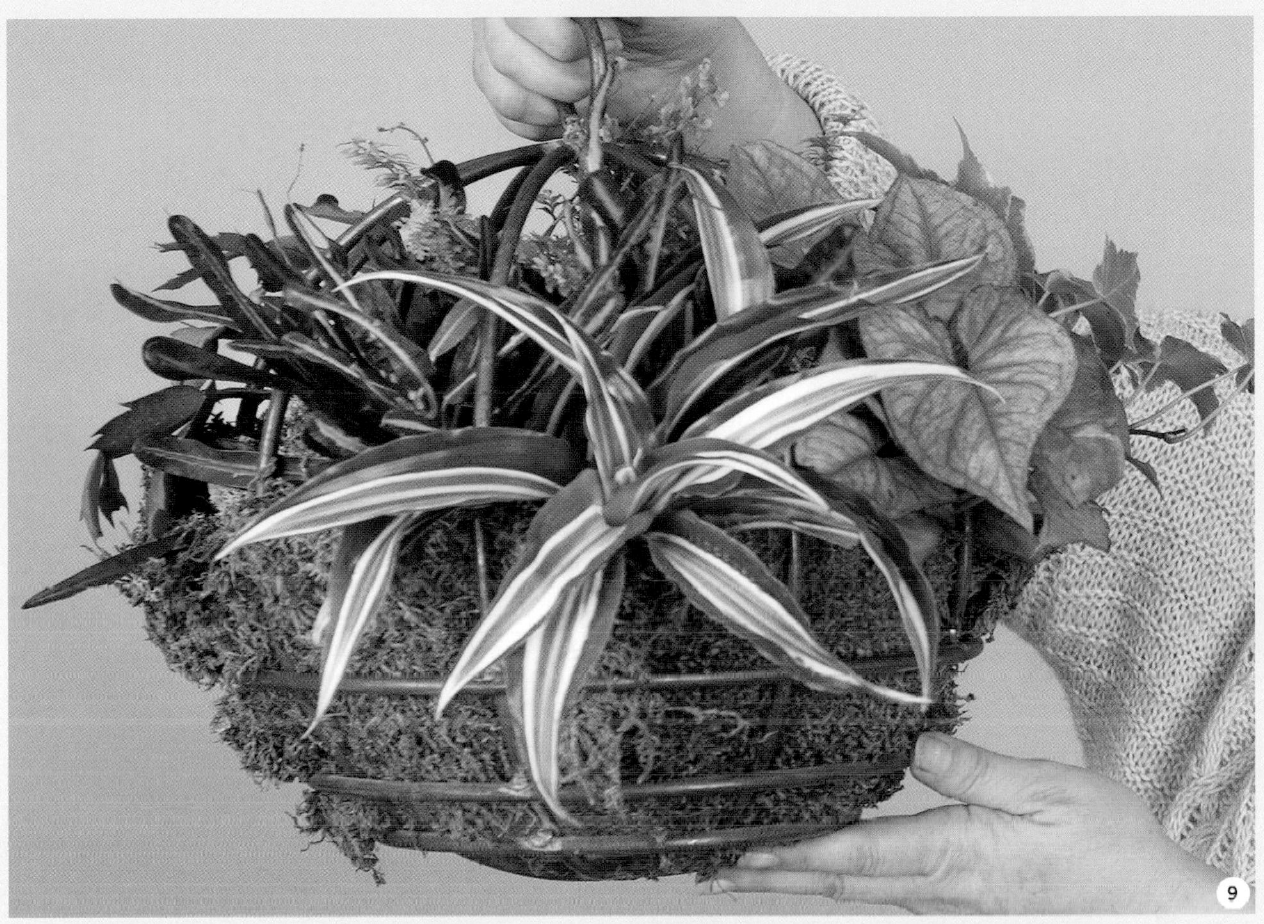


**9.** There you have it, your bundle of plant perfection. Hold it up and inspect your finished beauty. Watch it the first few weeks and try to figure out when it needs water. Check to see that all plants are secure and take time to admire your design. Now all that is left to decide is where to hang your creation!

In New York City, flawless planters thrive on the most coveted spot for a houseplant collection: the windowsill. Meagan Rosson's cats have their own mighty built-in perches so they can view life outside without having to take away windowsill space from her plant collection. The mighty windowsill of Williamsburg, Brooklyn, is where her cats, Brooklyn and Mac, have a front-row seat to the Manhattan skyline.

## THE MIGHTY WINDOWSILL

Urban living makes the windowsill our largest houseplant service area. It brings needed sunlight and supplies to an area not already used for function. What does your mighty windowsill look like?

Windowsills are where sun, the source of life, comes indoors and where our plants can find a place to flourish. Here we can create a design to show off our collection or we can choose to pile a jumble of greenery, growing one over the other.

How many houseplants can we jam on our sill? Does it have ample room to create a houseplant circus?

Small pots are at home on the windowsill. The spatial needs of the windowsill vary from apartment to home to office, but you can most likely find a pot that fits nicely on the ledge.

So, our job is to find plant trays or saucers with high sides/lips to house planters with drainage holes. It can be any sort of holder that will keep the water from dripping down the sill and all over the floor and furniture. Cramped city apartments leave less room for plants and pets to coexist, so the windowsill often becomes the coveted shared spot where the only unobstructed light is available.

Your windowsill can be perfection or a cluttered mess of tropical leaves, or your windowsill can be a carefully selected collection of cactus genera. The design of plants and planters can also be dictated by the room or office space itself, or your

particular likes. Do you live in a modern high-rise apartment or a California mission-style bungalow? Is your style industrial, modern, or rustic? Architecture influences how you create your windowsill assortment in your space.

Let your own sense of self create your design style. It may take time to find your aha moment. You may find yourself carrying your tall fiddle-leaf fig from room to room before you finally say, "Aha, now that looks good." The same can be said of your windowsill. Try different plants to see how colors, shapes, and sizes fit together. Vary the leaf shapes of the plants and sit different heights next to one another so your eye flows across the sill from plant to plant. As you stare at your sill, something may just look out of place, so go with your gut and move it to another location. You don't have to be an interior designer to know when something looks off center.

My kitchen windowsill faces westward and from there I see the most colorful sunsets in summer. It's a desirable sill because it is at eye level and I can peer effortlessly into my small terrarium worlds filled with air plants, seashells, and moss.

Amelie Segrestan of My Little Greens, a Brooklyn succulent design service, chose a lovely copper-covered planter grouping to enhance this cherry wood window frame. Because of the monochromatic pots, Amelie mixed the sizes of the pots and plants. Here *Crassula* jade and *Haworthia* are flanking a wonderful *Agave* in center stage. It looks like a hazy summer day in the Big Apple. Haze and pollution can block out a portion of the sun's intensity, which affects the amount of light plants receive.

I once went to a bird of prey flight demonstration and witnessed a great horned owl flap its wings for a good stretch while perched on the arm of its handler. Now on my mighty windowsill sits a tiny plastic owl peering out at me from inside a glass globe. Who? Yes, you.

## WINDOWSILL AND WATERING

You would assume that the sun shines straight onto a windowsill, yes? This is another spot where you must assess the intensity of the light, the direction the sun is shining, the time of day, and the duration of light through the window.

Many houseplant instructions suggest indirect lighting for indoor plants because in some geographical areas the sun shines red-hot (such as deserts, southern California, or the Mediterranean) and is too much for plants.

On the northeast coast, here in New York State, I like to offer direct sunlight to certain botanicals in my windowsill collection. If I see the necessity, as they are wilting or have a burnt leaf, I will shade the plants a bit in June and July. During the summer, the sun sets well into the evening at 9:00 p.m.—that is a long, hot day. I consistently put my air plant–filled glass globes and small succulents in direct sun, which help them grow large and robust.

The one factor I make sure to provide is sufficient water. The kitchen windowsill is a spot I see on my daily routine, so I can ensure the water threshold is consistently met. While I'm washing dishes or cooking, I love watching my collection grow. Having plants near the sink makes it easy to give them a bit of water at any moment the plants seem too dry. I keep a mister nearby to give the air plants a good, heavy mist at least twice a week.

Have I lost a plant or two over the years? Well, yes—haven't we all? Life and living things are subject to many factors during their existence. Sometimes these factors create a moment when survival is compromised and their demise is unstoppable. I try to keep this from happening if I can. You can too, by following the information on threshold watering on page 21.

BELOW: A larger windowsill full of late-day sunlight can hold the extended fronds of the grand Boston fern (*Nephrolepis exaltata*). All the greenery looks so happy here in the sunlight, giving off positive vibes.

OPPOSITE: Isn't this collection of cement pots and succulent cuttings perfect? They come from Christie Lothrop of MadPotters. Gold accents look great on the planters sitting on the pristine white windowsill. Here a simple three-tier, tall-to-short arrangement is ideal. The jumble of succulents is terrific in shades of green and bluish tones.

Green life is so inviting when the outdoors are cold and wintery. We can hide with our greenery until springtime calls us outside.

## HANGING IN FRONT OF WINDOWS

Honestly, I get such a thrill out of watching baby spider plants (*Chlorophytum comosum*) grow in midair and dangle down off their mother plant. The sunlight shining through their delicate flowers and slivers of green and white leaves is delightful.

For many reasons, you will want to hang plants in your window: Your sill may be so thin that only tiny pots or an air plant can sit there. Or maybe you want to capitalize on the natural light so your plants will thrive. The biggest reason to hang plants is to build your tropical forest upward.

## HANGING GLASS GLOBE REVOLUTION

The outstanding glass globe is full of possibilities for an endless number of creations. Inside this world seems to be the remnants of the sea, bits of blue coral, seashells, and sand. Are you straight away transported to the ocean and its inhabitants?

The revolution of the glass globe is remarkable. It is the dearest vessel of the terrarium world. Whatever you put into this encompassing glass world appears wonderful. I prefer to mimic what I see in nature or what I remember to be the natural world. Beauty—and their memory of it—is in the eye of the beholder. Sometimes I use materials that I have foraged along my travels—memoirs from another place I would love to be right now. Terrarium worlds take me away.

Hanging glass globes have revolutionized terrarium-making by creating a portable glass house that can hang on its own in a window, join a grouping on a table runner, or sit next to lit candle votives that create a sparkling display. Their sizes and styles run the range of shapes, from round, oval, pear, and teardrop, and from three inches to eight or more. Many house only air plants and gravel, while others have succulents piled inside. Air plants really enjoy this environment; mine do well inside globes of any shape. This also makes them the absolute easiest to care for with the squeeze of a water mister. The sand absorbs the water runoff on the air plant and our epiphyte *Tillandsia* friends stay dry and happy.

One of the newest terrarium trends is the stand for the hanging glass globe. This size is terrific for your desk because it takes up less space. You can peer into the Jurassic Park of your imagination and get lost. Weren't you concentrating on work a minute ago?

# OVAL GLASS
## STEP-BY-STEP

One is filled like a tropical jungle complete with a white river of pebbles; another includes a home for an air plant. Enjoy the assembly in the oval shape. You will want to start making various landscape environments and line them up in an impressive collection of terrarium nirvana. There is that cute factor!

### MATERIALS

- Oval glass globe
- Gravel (small, natural color)
- Potting soil
- Sheet moss (green, dried/preserved)
- Small, teak long-handled shovel (or an iced tea spoon)

### PLANT SELECTION

- *Neanthe bella* palm (mini parlor palm)
- *Kalanchoe tomentosa* (panda plant)
- *Tillandsia andreana* (air plant)

1. Add a bit of soil to the bottom of the glass globe as a base for the plant to sit upon. I reduced the soil rootball to help the palm fit into its new home, as it is a bit tall for the space. When planting your first specimen into the globe, especially if it is tall, it helps to put the leaf head in first and upward into the globe. This angle makes it easier to push the plant into placement at the rear of the globe. Let's see if it fills in the scene in the globe.

2. The panda plant should tilt out the opening a bit so we can see the interesting fuzz and brown spots of this *Kalanchoe*. In this case, I put the rootball in first and backed it up against the rootball of the palm so they fit snugly together.

3. Tilt the globe back a bit so gravity will help the soil fall into the small opening. You do not want the soil all over your greenery, so you must use a tool to assist you. I love using my teak long-handled terrarium tools. The handles are smooth and thin, which makes it easy to hold them between your fingers. You can use kitchen spoons, long-handled iced tea spoons, or milkshake spoons. I do not advise you use your fingers, or you will see the soil spreading wildly in a mess.

4. My trusty teak long-handled mini shovel is the perfect size to slide alongside the plants. Tilt the shovel away from the plants and toward the glass to dump a spoonful of soil. Place the shovel as far back as you can without disturbing the plants so you can get a spoonful of soil in the rear of the globe.

5. Shovel spoonfuls of soil all around each plant and in the back until you cover the rootballs completely. If the ball is not covered, you risk the plant drying out and dying too quickly. A plant should be planted correctly, even in this small environment.

4

5

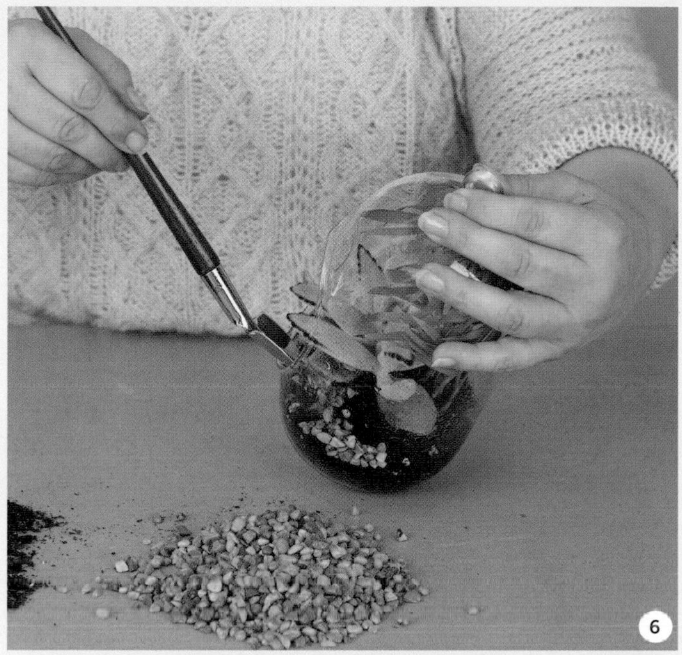

6. Now that we have sufficiently covered both rootballs with soil, we can move on to our topdressing. Again, tilt your globe and have gravity help to pour the small gravel into the globe. Gravel and pebbles tend to roll and tumble into the globe, so pour slowly so as not to accidently crack the glass. Use a stick to move the gravel into the back of your globe to cover the surface soil. Repeat until you like what you see. In this terrarium, the topdressing is decorative and less about the landscape we might we mimicking; it just makes the scene look appealing.

7. Adding an air plant to any terrarium creates a small point of interest. Air plants have a creature-like presence, like an insect or sea creature you added to your landscape scene. Here I added a *Tillandsia andreana* because it has a delicate, thin leaf structure. It is light and airy tucked into the space on the side. You will only need to mist this little creature; the humid air will do the rest. The other two plants will need a few streams of water shot directly into the rootballs once per week. Do not be fooled into thinking the water will last indefinitely in a glass globe. They have a large opening where the moisture evaporates, so have your mister ready nearby.

8. There you have it! Decorative living decor that you made yourself! Easy, fun, and lovely. Be a showoff and show off your newest craft.

# MOSS WALL ART PRESERVED

## MOSS LOVE

"A rolling stone gathers no moss" is an old proverb that refers to people who are always moving, with no roots in one place or another, avoiding responsibilities and cares. Verdant moss with no actual plant roots has been living on this planet since the dawn of plant life, which is almost forever.

Everyone seems to be saying, "More moss, please!" There are multitudes of full-time installation businesses around the world, such as Garden Beet of Melbourne, Australia, or Benetti MOSS of Italy, and FlowerBox Wall Gardens in the US. Crews work hour upon

A simple clump of living forest moss sitting under a glass cloche is enchanting. Wild plant life in my home is paramount for me. Add a few fake painted quail eggs and a natural wonder evolves right in front of your eyes.

hour to cover corporate lobby walls with moss, living or preserved. You may even find yourself lucky enough to dine in a restaurant that has created fabulous moss art on its walls.

Amazing moss designers can do even more with clever crafts—Artisan Moss in northern California creates inspired hanging moss creations; Sarah SK, known on Instagram as @rose.and.vine, creates anything from the Batman symbol to Charlie Chaplin's silhouette in moss on wood frames and more. These grand-scale living decor trends *can* all creatively translate into your living spaces on a smaller scale.

Have I already expressed my deep adoration for moss? Let me share with you more reasons. Moss is pliable and easy to shape, cut, glue, or pile into glass containers or top off potted plants. Moss allows our creativity to flow as we add it to our tabletop gardens or, yes, our hanging glass globes, and especially kokedama moss balls.

I was working with several bags of living Tennessee forest moss and kept it fresh in my refrigerator. Moss will last for weeks in plastic bags with tiny holes poked out to let condensation escape. If the baggie gets really wet, wipe it out with a paper towel. I place a palm-sized clump of moss in a glass bowl, jar, or terrarium and watch the intricate fern-like leaves. Moss belongs in the forest, not in my refrigerator, and yet there I store it until I plan a project.

## A THOUGHT ABOUT CONSERVATION

Is there enough moss growing on this earth to feed the moss frenzy we now experience? I worry when a precious living species on our spinning green planet becomes the object of desire to billions of humans inhabiting this world. So, conserve our precious moss and use every bit you collect or buy. Waste none!

## MOSS IDENTIFICATION

Thousands of moss species live worldwide, providing carbon offset along with trees. Moss is one of the oldest terrestrial plants on earth. I like to think of it growing at the feet of a massive brontosaurus.

A variety of mosses are preserved or dried for florists, crafts, and event displays. Craft projects come to life with each different form of moss. Many companies dye moss colors such as pink, chartreuse, blue, and purple, making for a creator's rainbow heaven.

Moss is available by the bag. Each type of moss brings a different texture and can fit into a variety of projects. Here are three types of moss you'll find most useful in craft projects.

- **Reindeer moss:** I find this to look a bit like sea coral. If your batch grows dry, it can become brittle. You should lightly mist the moss bunches with water to revive and soften them for use. This moss has shades of dark and light green, with which you can create a subtler design within a larger a moss design.
- **Spanish moss:** This moss is related to the epiphyte family of plants, which live on trees, such as orchids or air plants. Spanish moss dangles off giant oaks in the Southern states. Follow a winding driveway lined with oak trees of the Old South plantations and you will find Spanish moss in its natural habitat and natural gray color. Spanish moss looks like wiry hair and gives a particular look to any project you add it to.
- **Mound moss:** This variety is often used to create hillside terrain in a terrarium design with rocks larger than pebbles that mimic boulders. So many talented terrarium landscape artists utilize this moss effectively. Try using it in a flat tray alongside white sand for an Asian-inspired Zen garden.

Sheet moss creates a groundcover for *Peperomia puteolata*, a real plant love of mine. It grows so interestingly with four striped leaves, which shoot up tier after tier like a tower.

TOP LEFT: Design mixology at its best! A desk full of pop culture fun includes jumbled Scrabble letters and a few rubber stamps waiting to press notes onto heart cards for sweet messages. Proudly displayed in the middle of it all is my natural frame filled with heart-shaped sheet moss. Love is in the mix.

BOTTOM LEFT: Dyed lime green reindeer moss puffs out from this plain wooden frame, as if clusters of stone-hard coral were fit together like a puzzle. If you pat your finger across the moss, it is soft and spongy.

RIGHT: Moss piled high as a centerpiece makes this an even dreamier setting. Try pushing a few lit votive in glass candle holders down into the soft moss bed for a flicker of light at your table. You can add flowers, such as daisies or violets, to beautify the setting.

## MOSS BOTANY SIMPLIFIED

Here is a quick, simple botany lesson on moss. Moss is broken into two types or classifications: *pleurocarpous* and *acrocarpous*. Pleurocarpous moss grows outward with tiny branches, as if it is slowly creeping around. Acrocarpous moss grows upward into neat, thick little mounds of tightly packed stems. Understanding the growth pattern of the moss you intend to use in your living decor will give you a better idea of how to use and care for it.

For example, sheet moss, a common type used in craft projects, is a pleurocarp and has a flat growth habit. The thatch bottoms of pleurocarps attach well to stone, making them better for colonizing on hard surfaces.

Have you seen or heard of mound moss (*Dicranum scoparium*, often called mood moss)? Mound moss is an acrocarp, which forms mounded colonies and has an upright growth habit. Acrocarps are slow growers compared to the pleurocarps.

Moss has no true root system and can therefore live on many surfaces. If you walk in a woodland area, you will find moss growing on rocks, bark, in crevices, and on the ground. Moss is drought tolerant and takes moisture from rain, humidity, and even fog, while absorbing dotted sunlight through tree canopies.

The tiny green structures of moss do not produce flowers, pollen, or seeds, so how do they reproduce? After fertilization they develop sporophytes, which are mini stalks topped with single capsules that contain spores.

Here a tiny *Alocasia* flourishes as a single plant in a terrarium with its roots buried in living moss piled upon a bedrock of pure white cut granite. Both the moss and plant live happily in the moist habitat.

PROJECT

# MOSS JAR GARDENS
## STEP-BY-STEP

I like to make simple jar gardens using supermarket tomato sauce jars, particularly from companies that use Atlas Mason jars. Here's how I do it.

1. Clean the jars thoroughly. Toss in your decorative gravel, pebbles, or glass marbles of choice to sit at the bottom of the jar. This creates a space where excess water can drain away from plant roots and evaporate upwards, feeding the plant's need for constant moisture. The material you use for the bottom layer creates a decorative element you can match to the plant's colors or your room's decor.

2. Try placing a barrier made out of paper cut exactly to the interior size of the container. Place the paper over the gravel or pebbles to keep soil, sand, or moss from sifting into your colorful bottom layer. I like to keep layers clear and separate because you can see them through the glass jar. This is a good overall design practice.

3. Take a chunk of your living moss in your hand. Do not pull out slivers of it because you want to keep a good measure of the thatch mat intact to hold the moss together. Form it so the green side hits the glass and the brown side is facing inward or down. Leave a space or hole in the center to fit a small terrarium plant with a rootball about 1 inch wide.

4. Find your favorite plant. I often use *Ficus pumila* (variegated creeping fig) or *Pellaea rotundifolia* (button fern) for this project. Both plants have thick leaves, are strong growers, and will be good candidates for the small living quarters.

5. Squeeze your plant's wet rootball and place it in the center of your forest moss bed. Tamp it down.

6. Pull the moss closely around the rootball using a tool such as a knife or chopstick to manipulate it. If you have the lid of the jar, screw it on. This will ensure the moisture does not escape and you will rarely have to water your new jar terrarium. You are done!

## EASY DIY WOODEN FRAME DESIGNS

This project is quick, easy, and sweet. Make several and create a display wall of moss. When completed, you can hang them together, add them to bookcases, or mix them in with other mossy projects. It makes a good rainy day project for children. The heart shape can be a loving Valentine's Day gift coupled with a houseplant and chocolates for your special plant lover.

There are three versions in this step-by-step project. I left the frames undecorated so you can see the natural wood. These frames can easily be painted, rubber stamped with a message, embellished with glitter, or designed in whatever style you want. You can create a complicated painted design, or apply floral stickers. Be a clever crafty maker.

When finished, keep your preserved moss wall frames out of direct sunlight. Strong sunlight fades color whether it is fabric, paint, or your lovely preserved moss wall art.

Finding shelf space for my works of preserved moss art among Lori Adams's absolutely perfect photographic art wall display!

## WARNING

Glue gun metal tips become very hot when heated up. As the glue squeezes out, it too is very hot. The glue will stick to your skin and burn because you cannot remove it quickly. Please be careful whenever using glue guns, especially around children.

PROJECT

# HEART FRAME
## STEP-BY-STEP

### MATERIALS

- Heart-shaped wood frame
- Reindeer moss (lime green, dried, preserved)
- Glue gun
- Extra glue sticks
- Scissors

1

2

3

1. Begin by picking out a portion of sheet moss large enough to cover the heart cut-out. Sheet moss can sometimes have a thick growth of thatch on the underside. You will want to pick out the flattest piece you have because it will fit in the frame much more easily.

2. Pull out the paper placeholder in the frame representing a photograph. This is your stencil to measure and cut a perfect replica of moss to add in place of a photo. I do this step freehand without any preliminary tracing. Hold the moss and paper tightly in your fingers. Begin cutting the moss on the side that is easier for you.

3. Slowly turn the stencil with the moss as you cut. Hold them tightly; if you let go, your moss will move and your perfect cut will be inaccurate. As you turn the set in your hand, continue to cut around the heart.

4

5

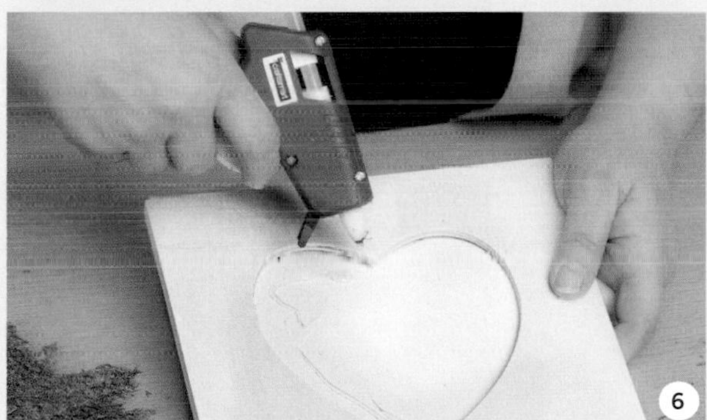

6

7

**4.** Cut close to the edge of the paper but not under it with the scissors. You can begin to see how it matches the paper. Repeat turning the set until you make your way all around the paper cut-out.

**5.** There you have a perfect moss heart cut-out. Put the paper back in the frame because it will be your base to glue the moss onto in the next step. Hold your moss cut-out up against the frame and see if you have cut too large or small, then make any necessary corrections. This is done *before* the glue is applied.

**6.** Apply a thick line of glue around the perimeter on the paper and additional glue dots in the center. Softly place the moss cut-out onto the hot glue. Hold your hand behind the frame and your other hand on top of the moss. Press lightly and hold until the glue has cooled and hardened.

**7.** Easy peasy! A sweet moss heart for yourself or your sweetheart.

PROJECT

# RECTANGLE FRAME
## STEP-BY-STEP

Reindeer moss comes in puffs, tufts, and balls. When I look at it, I see lime-colored coral. Most coral reefs are built from stony corals that consist of groups of polyps. Nature has a way of showing us its wonder. Let's mimic green coral—in a frame!

### MATERIALS

- Rectangular wood frame
- Reindeer moss (lime green, dried, preserved)
- Glue gun
- Extra glue sticks
- Scissors

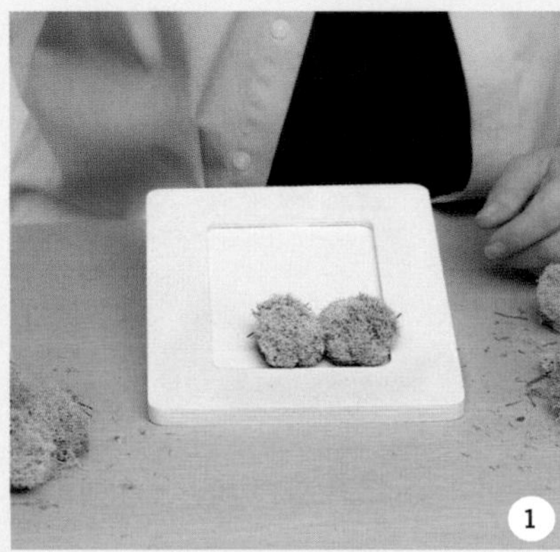

1

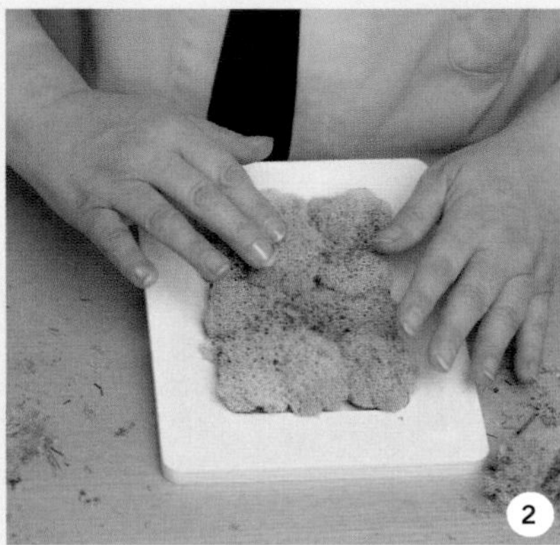

2

3

1. Pick out your favorite tufts with the form that speaks to you. Begin to arrange them inside the rectangular frame cut-out.

2. Rearrange the balls until you are satisfied with your collection. Mine fills up and spills over the cut-out interior edge, which is my intended effect.

3. Begin in the corner by picking up a moss ball and shooting it with a plop of glue. Then press down the piece until the glue cools and hardens.

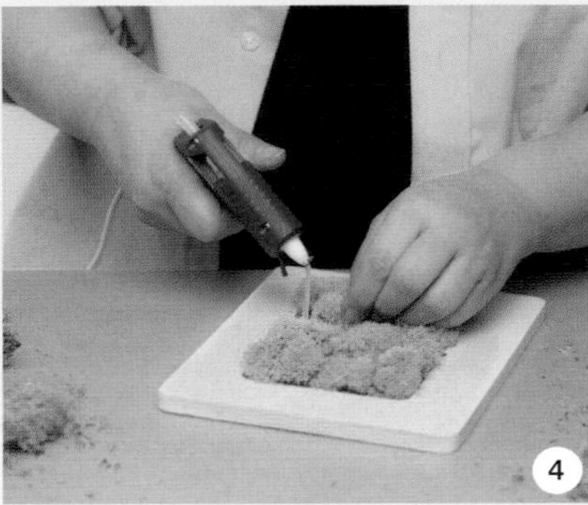

**4.** Repeat Step 3 with each loose moss ball until they are all glued into the frame.

**5.** Turn the frame around and pick up a moss tuft in the remaining corners. Add a plop of glue, then press down the piece.

**6.** Take a look at the puffs of moss and how they are glued together. Find any spaces or holes in the design, then pick out small pieces of moss and glue them in the gaps so there are no holes in the design.

**7.** Look at your frame now that all the spaces have been filled. As some of the tufts, puffs, and balls will be larger or irregularly shaped, you will want to give them a trim.

**8.** Fantastico! Your frame of coral-like lime moss is complete. Looks good! Now make five more and hang them two-by-two in a square on the wall, maybe over your bed. Moss art preserved forever.

PROJECT

# TRIPTYCH FRAME
## STEP-BY-STEP

Here we are working with reindeer moss again in a similar manner, but this frame does not require as much precision. It is a matter of stuffing all three sections with soft portions of moss.

### MATERIALS

- Wood frame with three square sections
- Reindeer moss (lime green, dried, preserved)
- Glue gun
- Extra glue sticks
- Scissors

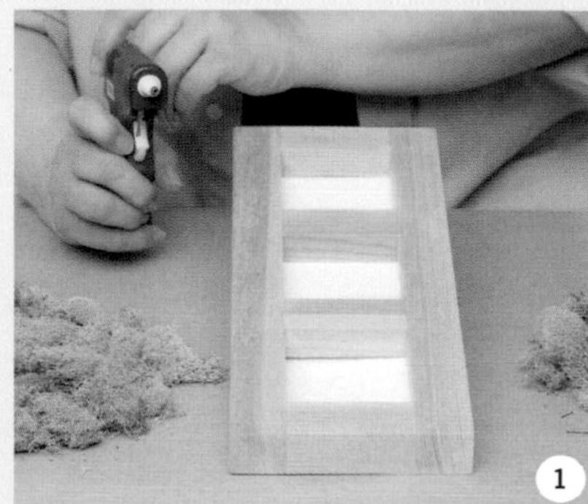

1

2

3

1. The shape of this frame may be easier to work with if it is propped up. You can slide a wood wedge or book under your frame. Use something that will not be of concern if damaged by the hot glue.

2. Pick out varying shades of your favorite green tufts. Begin to arrange them inside each small square cut-out. Begin in the corner by picking up moss and shooting it with a plop of glue. Then press down the piece until the glue cools and hardens.

3. Once enough moss is in the small cube, look for any spaces and holes. Hold a tiny piece of moss in one hand and squeeze hot glue into the space. Then immediately press the moss into the space. Hold until the glue cools and hardens.

**4.** Repeat the same process for the middle cube. An alternate method would be to hold the moss ball over the cube, squeeze glue onto the moss ball, and then immediately place it into the section. Hold until the glue cools and hardens.

**5.** Before you complete your last cube, compare the shades to the other two cubes. If you want to swap out some pieces, do so before you glue.

**6.** Repeat the same process for the last cube. Always add a spot of glue into the spaces and holes in the design as you add bits of moss to fill the cubes to fullness. Look at each cube and press down any moss that may loosen.

**7.** Bravo! You have now completed your triptych of cubes. Some of the moss is slightly different shades of green, which looks terrific. This shade difference creates a color design throughout the three squares.

# ANATOMY OF A PLACE SETTING

BELOW: The fern's fiddlehead rises out of the plant's center and unfurls ever so slowly as spring comes upon us in the same manner. Spring's trumpeters tell us life renews.

BELOW RIGHT: Menu: *Déjeuner de fraises rouges et de tranches de fromage.*

OPPOSITE: What a magnificent way to spend an afternoon! If you cannot rent a mansion, you can recreate a dreamy table setting in your own home. The idea is to include plants right on the table with your plates. You can use vines draped across or wound in a circular shape to mimic a wreath. I like the rich green color of English ivy (*Hedera helix*). You can either buy a plant with long tendrils and cut them off, or use the plant as-is in the center of the table.

## FLORIBUNDUS SPRINGTIME

Spring! New, green fiddleheads unfurl up out of the grown—dark, cold winter fades, and brown, empty gardens sit waiting to burst. Why not bring this moment of renewal to life? How about planning a simple brunch in a dreamy conservatory overlooking a formal garden? *Oui*!

## ENTERTAINING WITH BOTANICALS

Nature inspires. Spring rain brings color back to grassy lawns and bursts opens the leaves on the trees. Let the season bring houseplants to your table. Order a bagful of living moss and sit down to a meal where you can touch, smell, and see the season at your place setting.

It is such a treat to spend a day in this room at the Bartow-Pell Mansion Museum. I teach terrarium-building workshops in the mansion's conservatory room. We sit around a table fiddling with plants and soil as we gaze out at the garden. If you open the doors in summer, you can hear the gurgling fountain. One day, I saw deer in the woods; they were two bucks with enormous racks of antlers. This is the Bronx!

I have hiked and biked through these lands and found a place about people and events from a time long ago. It inspired me to create this café-style table setting. I often let my surroundings guide me toward a design. I look around and ask myself, "How do I feel in this place? What do I know about this place?" I begin to build around that expression.

In this conservatory room, I saw an opportunity to use ferns. Ferns were very popular in the Victorian era (roughly 1937 to 1901, the period of Queen Victoria's reign). During this time, a popular practice was to house ferns and orchids in a Wardian case, a popular style glasshouse terrarium. The British have a name for the fern craze of the time, called *Pteridomania*. The Pteridophyte taxon includes ferns—it basically refers to a group of plants that reproduces by spores.

Fern crazy we will go! In the nearby woods, I can easily find ferns. I choose to use maidenhair ferns (*Adiantum*) because of their soft leaves that move in the breeze. They drape themselves over their planters' edges for a delicate visual. Warning: Maidenhair ferns will try the patience of even the most devote caretaker. You must keep the soil soggy wet and mist them constantly! Treat them as if they were living in a stream.

## ABOUT THE BARTOW-PELL MANSION MUSEUM

The historic nineteenth-century Bartow-Pell Mansion Museum is a gem of a time capsule in which the Pell family lived in a world complete with a conservatory room, wall-to-wall windows, and French doors that open to a formally designed garden. The property is tucked into a corner of Bronx, New York. This land has passed through the hands of the Native American Siwanoy people, Ann Hutchinson, and even the Continental Army.

The mansion sits on Pelham Bay Park, owned and maintained by New York City, and claims acreage larger than Manhattan's Central Park. There are bike paths, horseback-riding bridle paths, and hiking trails to explore right in the heart of the Bronx borough. You can ride your bicycle to the nearby thirteen-mile saltwater shoreline, Orchard Beach, which hugs the Long Island Sound.

I kept it simple to show off the plates, but it really needs fern-inspired cloth napkins, silverware, and creamy pats of butter to smear on the muffins. You can imagine all you would like to eat at your botanically decorated feast. *Bon appétit*!

Living decor is for entertaining as well as everyday decor. Scour home decor shops for theme-patterned dinnerware that add to the ambiance of the moment you choose to create. There are many different themes, especially since *Monstera deliciosa* came onto the scene. Your soiree can be for a holiday or a season and the plants can mimic the occasion. This luncheon-style table setting includes a *Monstera*-shaped felt coaster and the leaf is used as a cut flower.

This is my dream. Here I can imagine my life far away from the hustle and bustle of my busy life in a room full of weeping fig trees (*Ficus benjamina*), citrus trees, and large Boston ferns (*Nephrolepis exaltata*).

## MONSTERAMANIA

I own a wonderful book by Sarah Whittingham entitled *The Victorian Fern Craze*. In it, she describes how ferns were so popular in the 1850s that their images appeared on buildings, carpets, and greeting cards.

Does that sound familiar? Maybe a century from now, our time will be referred to as Monsteramania and we will be called *Monstera* collectors! We might not even have to wait that long—Monsteramania is upon us now! I'm hooked and have redecorated my home with placemats, tea towels, table runners, and melamine plates. I'm looking into wallpaper for the bathroom. Everything *Monstera*!

# PICKING PUMPKINS AUTUMNAL CENTERPIECE

Welcome to my autumnal afternoon tea party! Join me, won't you, in this fabulous space for a hot cup of Sri Lankan tea and warm popovers fresh out of the oven. I've set out my ceramic pumpkin sugar and creamer set, pumpkin plates, and thrown in some twinkling lights to make us feel festive. I'll show you how to make a pumpkin-themed centerpiece of your own on the next page.

After you spend an afternoon on a farm where pumpkins' growing journey began, you feel compelled to give them a proper decorative exhibition. Our Hudson Valley squash-family gourds traveled to reach our table. This is a collection that fits easily on a coffee table, buffet, or front hall table for a seasonal display of houseplants, ceramics, and pumpkins!

Now you can create your own. Jump to the project on the next page and look at how easy it can be! I am going to show you exactly how to build this pumpkin-inspired centerpiece. Once you see the building blocks of each stage, adding another houseplant or decor piece with every layer to fill the rectangular-shaped table along the center runner, it's straightforward.

The pumpkin topper will last weeks for your enjoyment. Bring some friends over and have a social gathering. They will want to know how you did it! That pumpkin is adorable with its foliage topper.

PROJECT

# PUMPKIN CENTERPIECE
## STEP-BY-STEP

1. We begin with our dearest pumpkin with her air plant plume and set her centerstage.

2. Pick one side to begin your balancing game. At this point, anything is possible, so I use a plain undecorated pumpkin to accompany Ms. Plume.

3. I chose the plate because it is flat and I am not sure where it will fit properly. For now, it is a placeholder in our balancing act. Anything can be moved as we go along. Find a spot to start the motion.

4. My *Aloe* fits perfectly in this attractive marbleized terracotta pot. I am intentionally placing the *Aloe* behind and flanking Ms. Plume to add another element of height. Think of each object as a steppingstone to the one next to it—do they complement each other?

5. I try placing smaller objects in front of the large pumpkin where I know they won't obstruct the view of it. The pumpkin sugar and creamer set are sweet sitting in front of the real thing.

6. This is a runner display; it is wise to keep the display tight and wide. Each object can be added in a string left and right next to the previous object. I nestle the burlap bee skep behind the ceramic sugar bowl. Notice that it connects with the *Aloe* pot, because both are brown.

7. Here I have a cascading English ivy plant. I can pull its tendrils a bit over the plate to give the objects a visual connection. In our steppingstone pattern, I have a spot for two small gourds to further connect our plate with the ivy. Slide your gourd right in front but back a bit to give a little depth of focus. The second mini gourd sits just right of our center focal point. Hop from one object to another along the rectangle runner.

8. Now I've jumped back to the left side. I have an interesting *Croton* that has thin, tall, green leaves colored with red, orange, and yellow. This color combo is perfect for our array of shades and it matches the spiky growth pattern of the *Aloe*. At this point, you can begin to see the shapes fitting in nicely next to one another. I push the bee skep over a bit to the left to introduce the planter. The planter is terracotta, so it keeps with our orange theme.

9

10

9. We are so close to completion, but I see something is missing. We have filled our gaps between each object with an overlapping steppingstone effect, but there are still gaps and white spaces. Look between the creamer and sugar bowl, where there is still too much white space. I have the perfect thing to fill it, and it's a living thing—another air plant with a plume matching our pumpkin topper can sit on the table between our small ceramics. Yes, we must add a string of lights. Stretch out the string and place it along the edge of the fabric runner to hide any gaps and to add shine. Behind our table are the fantastic shelves full of art that could use even more illumination. As we look from table to shelves, we are almost overstimulated with all we can see visually in our studio party room. It brings us closer to complete and oh so pretty.

10. Here, a final look at our festive table full of seasonal living decor and houseplants with beloved objects. Each object holds its own memory of where it was found on my way through life. You can make this the bar of your party, with bottles of German Riesling wine and craft local beer—maybe a light autumn ale, pale and refreshing. How about adding a ceramic terracotta-colored container for ice with bottles of sparkling water? You can add plates of food as your guests help themselves to a treat, then sit down yourself to an afternoon of chatter and laughter!

# SUCCULENT PUMPKIN
## STEP-BY-STEP

Most YouTube tutorials similar to this project will suggest using succulent cuttings that can be ordered online. That is easier. If you make your own, you would have to cut the stems from the rootball of a small succulent and let them heal and dry for a day or two. In an unconventional manner, I use mini potted succulent plants. This makes use of the plants' roots, which helps them survive longer on top of the pumpkin.

### MATERIALS

- Medium- to small-sized pumpkin
- Spanish moss (natural gray or dyed green, dried and preserved)
- Glue gun
- Glue sticks
- Water mister
- Scissors

### PLANT SELECTION

Mini succulent varieties:

- *Echeveria*
- *Crassula*
- *Hoya* rope
- *Tillandsia*

1. Begin by picking a pumpkin that has the smallest stem possible. If there is a large stem on the top of your pumpkin, you will need to saw it off—pumpkin stems are surprisingly tough woody vines that attach the pumpkin to the rest of the plant. I sawed the stem off the one I used in this project and even that was a herculean effort.

2. Before you apply the hot glue, have your Spanish moss ready to plop on top. The glue dries quickly and you want to be prepared. Pull a portion of moss out of the bag and tug it apart a bit until it is nice and loose. Apply a dollop of hot glue to the pumpkin and press the moss into place until the glue cools.

3. Now prep the plants by loosening the soil from the rootball. Remove as much as you can, almost to the bare root. This will make inserting the plants' stems into the moss base easier. Mist the roots or sit them in water for a moment before planting them.

4. Plan where you will place each plant on top. Think about how you will view this pumpkin when it is complete. If you plan to view it from the front, you may want to tilt the plant head a bit forward so you view the lovely circular rosette on top.

5. Now all your materials are ready to glue in place. Begin by gluing down the focal point plant. Repeat this step clockwise around the focal point plant with your other selections. You will begin to see a pattern come into play as your design vision takes shape.

4

5

6. If you managed to bare-root a plant, this segment can be inserted into a space between plants in the moss hair. Add a bit of glue and then slide the cutting into place. Hold the cutting for a moment and let the glue dry. Tug it slightly to make sure it holds tight.

7. Look for holes in the design. Decide which plant or material you have brought to the project that would fit nicely and would add interest to the bouquet. I had an air plant with a wonderful feather-like tuft of leaves that looked like a cardinal bird's head. I tested how it would look if I added it to the top center with its tuft facing upward.

8. Quite pleased with the spacing, I grabbed my glue gun and hit a few drops down. With my air plant in place to be pressed down and secured to the moss, I nuzzled it a bit into the grouping of plants. I wanted to make sure it will sit atop the pumpkin like a feather on a hat.

9. Trim off any loose Spanish moss that is hanging down. Clean up the design. Maybe prune off a leaf or two if you feel they seem to be sticking out of the tight grouping.

10. We are almost there, and our design has come together very well. If you feel the need to add a bit of water to each cutting, do so at this time. This is also how you will add some water over the next few weeks to keep the planting fresh and alive.

11. There she is! Pumpkin Princess shows off her wonderful autumnal hat complete with feather tuft. She is ready for the party placement, center stage.

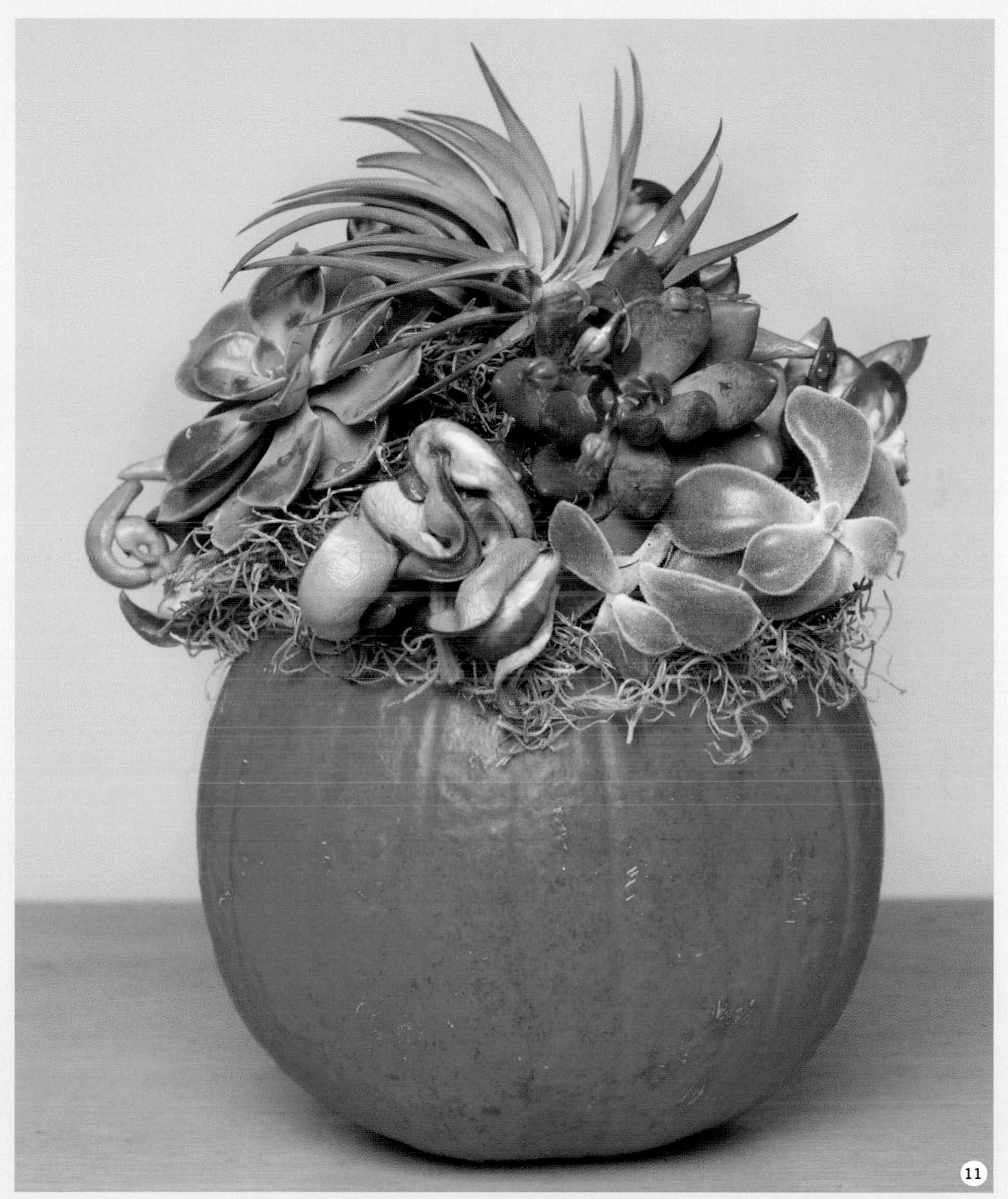
11

# TERRARIUM GEOMETRY & EVOLUTION

BELOW: This geodesic dome holds pristine white sand and pebbles that show off *Haworthia*'s white stripes. The dome has soldered gold metal stripes holding the pentagon glass segments together, which add a superior design.

OPPOSITE: Terrarium geometry and evolution are on display in this collection full of air plants, succulents, foliage plants, anything you like! Terrarium geometry personified.

## GEOMETRIC TERRARIUMS

Terrarium evolution is exciting. There are so many artisans designing and creating glass structures for your purchasing excitement. It seems that never before has the craft grown to this superb integrity of artistic fervor. What's the allure of terrariums? Their loveliness, of course! They are small, portable, and easy to create, and need very little attending, if any at all. What could be better than a bit of nature where you can view your miniature green world every day?

Handmade geometric terrariums can be bought online from anywhere worldwide. Find some vendors in the resources on page 160 to peruse and purchase new glass holders to decorate your spaces. You can experiment with your own ideas and create miniature conservatories.

COLLETTI

Even an empty dodecahedron terrarium looks good as a prop or a bookend. Fill it with chocolate kisses and place it on your coffee table. Such a vessel is elegant whether empty or filled with juicy succulent plants.

Terrarium geometry includes a list of names that a math whiz can appreciate. A dodecahedron terrarium is twelve-sided and each glass segment is a pentagon (five sides). In small geodesic planters, you can recreate the Earth's deserts, tropical rainforests, or moss woods. Geodesic domes can be the basis of geometric terrariums or tiny biodomes that accumulate humidity while still allowing it to escape out of the one open glass pane.

Real life-size biodomes have been built to create self-sustaining environments for creatures to live within them. Biosphere 2 is an experimental research facility owned by the University of Arizona and has been operating since 1991. The interior houses multiple environments that explore the possibility of humans surviving in an enclosed space.

The Montreal Biodome is a scientific museum that allows visitors to walk through four ecosystems found in the Americas, including a tropical rainforest, the Gulf of Saint Lawrence's marine life, and sub-polar islands.

I have spent a lifetime in the Enid A. Haupt Conservatory at the New York Botanical Garden, which opened in 1902. There you can find yourself engulfed in the heat of the beloved palm dome, where enormous tropical palm trees have lived for more than a century. You walk in and instantly feel the warm, humid air. After all these years, I still marvel at the experience. The giant structure gives you the personal connection of life within a terrarium. If you find an opportunity to take a stroll in a glasshouse conservatory, you will be impressed by the landscape of each glasshouse.

## WATER TERRARIUMS

A delicious design mixology of strawberries, cylinder terrariums, and our new interesting element under glass: water. Water terrariums are becoming a new, trendy, and experimental living decor creation to add to your collection. I found it easy to make a small one in no more than 30 minutes. Buy your plants at an aquarium shop; the very plants that live in a freshwater fish tank survive nicely in a water terrarium.

The cork-topped water terrarium just left of center is its own little world among the other open-air terrariums at this brunch table.

## LIGHT

I have been experimenting with how much light my Java fern (*Microsorum pteropus*) likes. You should only put a water terrarium on a windowsill if sunlight is minimal. Water heats up fast under glass as if a magnifying glass were held over the plants. As we go into summer, the sunlight will heat up the underwater plants in the glass jar. I opened the cork top to let heat escape and I saw a few deteriorated black leaves. So, I refreshed the terrarium by replacing the water. New, fresh water will improve the oxygen level; look for bubbles clinging to the leaves.

Now, my Java fern water terrarium lives in the bathroom with less direct sunlight. Like other ferns, the leaves have black spots on the undersides that are known as sporangia, or reproductive spores. Those black spots are natural and not a sign your plant is dying.

### WATER

Java fern, named after the Indonesian island, can be found in various parts of Asia. It commonly grows along streams, where it is found on wood or rocks at the river's edge, and where the humidity level is very high and the ground is quite wet.

Java fern does not want to be planted in soil, so gravel made a nice cover for the roots in the water. Java fern can also grow on driftwood, as long as the roots sit underwater. You do not have to submerge the entire plant underwater as some of the leaves can stick out of it.

The size of the water terrarium is entirely your call. Water is heavy and needs to be replaced periodically, so consider how much maintenance you wish to involve yourself in before you get started.

### DESIGN MIXOLOGY

While I continue to figure out the needs of my Java fern, I thought it looked magical on the springtime table buffet on the previous page. You can easily move this scene to your coffee table or dining table. Make several miniature aquatic terrariums and sit them together on a platter or on a runner down the center of the table with some greens, spinach leaves, or kale for an exotic display of imaginary sea algae.

## TERRARIUM TIPS

General instructions about moisture, condensation, and possible water requirements are the science of terrariums. The botany within is affected by the different styles of glass containers, designs that have lids or do not have lids, and whether there is a gasket on the lid. These subtle differences create the air circulation or air vacuum that will affect the growth of your plants and the maintenance needs of your terrariums.

## SAND-LAYERING TIPS

There are numerous approaches to building a sand terrarium, as well as a few important tips to follow to help deal with the sand material. One important lesson I have learned about sand is about the size of the crystal. Especially when using multiple layers of various colors, if one color of sand is too fine, then one color layer will blend into the other color below and create a sloppy mess. If you create a layered look with sand and pebbles, the sand must be on the bottom and the pebbles on top. The sand will fall through the pebbles and again create an indistinguishable muddle of materials. That just won't do!

When adding ingredients in a terrarium, I suggest using tools like household spoons and coffee scoops to add soil and such. I will include helpful instructions as you move along my project on page 136. You can build all sorts of distinctive styles and use many diverse shades of sand. This is where your own style and imagination kick in. How do you want your sand terrarium to stand out in a room?

My newest passion of terrarium style is creating layers of sand to enhance the view through the teardrop base. It is a bit of a challenge to keep the sand in place in dry terrariums while planting with small plants and their rootballs of soil. It takes surgeon-level skill to keep it contained. Practice creates perfected beauty.

# TERRARIUM MAINTENANCE

Within these slim glass cylinders you can see two terrarium concepts. The taller vessel houses three plants, *Asplenium nidus* (bird's nest fern), *Ficus pumila* (creeping fig), and a small fern variety. This sealed terrarium does not have the ability to ventilate excess humidity, so you can see some moisture condensation on the interior in the photo to the right. You should periodically wipe out this moisture with a paper towel and then put the plastic wrap back on tightly. If you do not wipe the interior, the water drops can build up and fall onto the leaves, which eventually will cause rotting. This simple maintenance task will make it right.

Layering is an additional concept that creates an attractive view through the glass. You can add a paper cut-out divider to create layers and keep the drainage material and the soil layers separate. A paper divider between every layer of gravel, soil, or pebbles ensures each remains clearly defined. Here the layering has occurred masterfully, as the divider itself is white paper and almost disappears. The layer of pristine white stones has no soil or moss mixed in because the divider is between. This will help to ensure you are an expert terrarium designer!

One of the best tips when designing terrariums is how to actually keep the inside glass area clean and uncluttered as you build your terrarium. Terrariums are created for the most part in glass containers, so, naturally, you see everything from the outside. As you add your gravel and soil, you must keep your small green plants clean so your final creation is an exquisite design.

Why is adding topdressing—such as gravel, pebbles, moss, seashells, or pinecones—significant in a terrarium? These are the materials that will define the real landscape you desire to mimic, whether it's your own private Idaho or the Petrified Forest of the Southwestern states.

ABOVE: These two slim terrariums are among my own favorites in my personal collection. Sometimes I put a simple, clear plastic sheet over the top of a repurposed glass vase. I literally *never* have to water these terrariums because the moisture inside recycles over and over again. This botanical science still mystifies me.

OPPOSITE: Here, I created two eco-environments in teardrop terrariums of two different sizes. Tropical plants include creeping fig, red-veined *Fittonia*, and *Kalanchoe tomentosa* (panda plant). The panda plant has a fuzzy texture to its leaves and is in the succulent family. I planted it at the open doorway so it would get the most air circulation and least moisture because I do not want its precious fuzz to deteriorate.

COOL

# GEODESIC TERRARIUM PLANTING
## STEP-BY-STEP

As you see, I started with two additional plants of the *Crassula* variety, but decided as I built the interior that the singular *Haworthia* should not have any other companions. As a result, the queen was elevated to such a special specimen on display in her gold geodesic throne. I also did not incorporate the chartreuse green reindeer moss. This is a good way to proceed. Bring many ideas to the table and let the process and natural beauty of the materials dictate your final design. Have fun creating your mathematically correct geometric terrarium of sand and stone!

### MATERIALS

- Geodesic glass container
- Sand (white) and pebbles (white)
- Seashells (conch)
- Spanish moss (green, dried, preserved)
- Scoops or long-handled teaspoons
- Chopsticks

### PLANT SELECTION

- *Haworthia*

1. It is always a good idea at the start to measure to see if your plants fit into the opening and how many plants you can plant together inside the container. You can move the plants around until you have decided on their placement. Look at the growth pattern of the plant. As you turn plants round and round, if one side of the plant looks better than the other or has a natural slant, then you will know which side to feature. Use this practice in your design to help you build and position the plants accordingly.

2. Start with a sand base. Try to pile more on the perimeter and create a slight center valley to plop your plant in the middle. You should pour the sand layer as high as possible, so you see it from the outside. It is all about what you see through the glass, so a half inch or 1 full inch can make a difference in the final outcome. It is difficult to remove the sand and plants as you progress, so slowly move through this process, stopping often to bend down to eyelevel with the terrarium to measure by sight if you have enough of the layer of sand.

3. Look through the glass to see if the plants are positioned exactly where you want to view them. In a geometric terrarium with many individual windows, you can sit the plant where it will be seen as if it were in a frame. When you are satisfied with its placement, add some more sand around the interior. You should notice the angle at which I hold the scoop. Always pour with the spoon or scoop pointing toward the glass wall and away from the plants. This will not only prevent the material from falling on the leaves but will help it to pile up against the interior glass walls.

4. After you finish pouring the sand, this is your opportunity to move the sand around. Repeat this process until you have covered the plant's rootball completely and have added enough sand to the base of your plant. You can alternate colors like the hills of New Mexico in Georgia O'Keefe's paintings, my inspiration of choice.

5. If you are satisfied with the level of sand and all soil has disappeared, now is the time for topdressing. Color is very critical in this style of design. Many times, I have piled on a scoop of pebbles and thought it did not look attractive, so I had to painstakingly take each pebble out. Save yourself this step by mixing your materials outside the container before you pour them inside. Again, the scoop is pointed away from the plant and toward the glass walls as I fill around the interior.

6. The lovely *Haworthia* is dead center and can be viewed right through the pentagon window. I have chosen to have the opening at the top, but you can tilt this container sideways and slide your hand through the open pane on the side to plant. The direction is entirely up to you and there is no right or wrong way. Let your own preferences guide you. Of course, you can always make multiples, with each in a different perspective.

7. Now I examine the terrarium to see where and how much more topdressing I may want to add. I am torn over whether to leave it simple or to test what looks more interesting. I still have my seashells and moss sitting on the table.

8. Here another variation with Spanish moss softly circling the *Haworthia* with one seashell positioned in front. It is also pretty and matches the overall design. Display the terrarium prominently in a brightly lit room.

## HERBARIUM BOTANICALS & CURATOR'S CORNER

I found this vintage print at a flea market for the perfect price point of $5. I cut it to size and slipped it in the back of the shadowbox frame. The two moths are real. I found them lying on the ground and carried them home carefully. They were sitting in a glass cup for a year before I got the idea to put them together on this print with hot glue. The moths are now part of my curatorial story of outdoor adventures, cherishing and exhibiting all of nature's living things.

An herbarium is a collection of preserved plant leaves with their Latin names, identification, and habitation. As a curator, I am fascinated by collections of the past. I will keep a pressed leaf, vintage print, or antique garden book for years tucked in a drawer. I press ferns from my hikes and frame them for display on the walls of my home. I take pride that I created my own fern herbarium, complete with proper botanical names and habitat information.

What came before the present time is beautiful to me. Combine my lifelong attachment to horticulture and botany with my education in anthropology and I become an amateur ethnographer. An ethnographer studies people and culture and the phenomenon of their existence. Why do people grow a certain plant or crop? Does it have meaning beyond the green? Is it magical, mystical, or spiritual? I want to know.

Sometimes I combine the old and new to bring a museum-like display to life. Let me share some vintage collectibles with you and ideas for how to display them. Pick a corner, shelf, or desk and begin a personal museum collection of artifacts you have found along your travels.

The term "cabinet of curiosities" emerged in the sixteenth century and defined a room of scientific objects rather than a cabinet—a natural history theater created of curious, odd living things that had not yet been categorized. There are numerous book collections with botanical illustrations of the time. This is my personal museum of curious objects.

TERRARIUMS
TERRARIUMS
TERRARIUMS
TERRARIUMS
TERRARIUMS

How about a cloche within a cloche? My husband, Daniel, gave me this glass box. He knows I will instantly use it as a mini glasshouse for a tiny plant. I am so lucky that he likes to live in a plant life museum.

## THE CLOCHE

The cloche began as a covering to protect plants from frost growing outdoors in the garden. Today, it has evolved to show off our objects of merit. Maybe a piece of quartz or a lovely orchid makes a beautiful ornamental decor piece. I had a few fake bird nests with eggs and thought they made a lovely spring statement. The cloche makes it easy to change up the exhibit in an instant. You can put together a little tropical plant garden in a dish and place a cloche over it. The tabletop garden is immediately raised above the norm with its glass bell jar cover.

Inside the small box sits a tiny *Cryptanthus*, one of the best terrarium plants. The *Cryptanthus* survives so well in humid air. The little glass box fits well under this glass dome. The dome securely fits into the groove cut in the wood base. A string of fairy lights makes it delightful. Many times, I add a book to my displays that helps tell its story. Here, coupled with the cloche, is a book on vintage prints. There on the cover is a botanical illustration of a fern's fiddle-leaf. Green plants, lights, and books all add up to a vintage storyline mixology.

## MACRAMÉ: NOT YOUR 1970S VERSION

Macramé has become a magnificent craft. Enormous wall hangings can be created for the home or office. Social media pictures explore gorgeous, intricately woven canopies, often used as a backdrop at wedding ceremonies. You can make your own macramé wall hangings in workshops.

Macramé plant hangers brighten up even the most dismal corner of any room.

The macramé piece on page 143 I found online; it measures 13 inches by 25 inches. I created this vintage print vignette with *Pteris* ferns, *Peperomia puteolata*, antique garden books, teak terrarium tools, and preserved vine. I started with the macramé as my centerpiece and worked clockwise to surround it with objects of soft green and brown tones. This is a living decor display that is easy to replicate on a shelf, mantel, or console table against a wall. It speaks to the herbarium curator with its botanical illustrator's vibe, and the representation is softened by the macramé.

## PEPEROMIA PUTEOLATA

*Peperomia puteolata* is a much-loved species by plant connoisseurs. The growth pattern is so interesting: the three or four whorled leaves of each tier have lovely white venation that draws outward from the stems. As the stems grow upward, a new level produces another leaf threesome or foursome. It continues this exquisite structure upward.

**LIGHT:** Being native to South America would suggest an environment for this plant that is humid with bright sunny days. You should provide a sunny window part of the day for a good dose of light to produce those towering petals. If your plant gets a bit leggy as it reaches for the light, pinch back one level of leaves to keep it bushy.

**WATER:** You must keep your *Peperomia*'s soil moist so the plant can support its tower climb upward. This plant is a good candidate for terrariums as it loves that warm, humid air. Keep it away from dry heat that will dry out the soil, or an air conditioner that will keep it too cool. Remember, south of the equator is hot and humid!

**DESIGN MIXOLOGY:** I chose this creamy off-white ceramic planter to pot up the *Peperomia* because of its lip that curls inward at the top. The *Peperomia* is planted lower down in the interior of the pot so that its tower of leaves pops up out of the top edge and spills over. The pot complements the macramé's color palette.

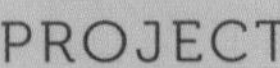


# MACRAMÉ DISPLAY
## STEP-BY-STEP

This tutorial will help you develop your styling skills. Follow along the pictures and see how the spaces and gaps are filled appropriately to create a complete houseplant display.

1. Start with an empty canvas. Take away distractions and build from an open area. This gives you a blank space to fill. If you had something there that you want to keep, take it away temporarily and add it back as you see the new big picture unfold.

2. Decide where and how you want to frame your display. How do you want to flank your design? It would be okay to have both hanging plants on one side. Either is a good design choice. Once you have your frame, you can begin to fill it in.

3. You can add a focal point to pull your eye into the center. For example, if the framed print on the wall is your hanging focal point, you can add an object on the table. The grate is a nice addition because it is not solid, so you can view the design against the plain painted wall. I added a small rectangular box on the left and a large pot of grass on the right. I continue to balance both sides in each step.

4. Let's start to fill in the left side of the frame. Have a taller plant in the background so that when you put smaller plants in the box they do not obscure the view of the rear plants. Are the objects spaced appropriately from one another? Keep adding and look at each added object to see if it fits and if you like how it completes the space.

5. Now, the right needs more plants. I had a tall, thin cactus that would slip into the space next to the pot of grass. If I didn't have this plant, I could leave the space empty, but would move the pot of grass to the left, a bit closer to the center grate to fill the gap (where the cactus would have been).

**6.** As you can see, I flanked the skinny cactus with two smaller succulents for balance, creating a trio overlapping the pot of grass and grate on the right side. On the left, I added a *Croton* in the box that lands right between the ZZ plant and arrowhead in the rear. Then, the white-striped *Dracena warneckii* sits directly to the right of the box, overlapping the grate connecting the focal point to the left side.

There are no more spaces or gaps, and no plants are obscured from view. If you run your eye from one end to the other, it flows from plant to plant because each object is linked together in an overlapping style. There are infinite versions of this design, but the point to this exercise is balancing the frame and filling in gaps between objects illuminating empty space. You will naturally be pulled into the center of the frame and then look side to side. If you find this style too formal or staged, in your display add additional memorabilia or throw in a few air plants. Continue to make an effort to balance the frame by placing items, living or not, in blank spots to keep it looking good. This is a simple method with an attractive final outcome.

## ART OF THE DISPLAY: A PHOTO STYLIST FLARE

Botanical styling can be simple. You can take an incredible plant and sit it on a pedestal in front of a prized photograph. Instantly, you have created a styled snapshot, like the one on page 150.

A photo stylist builds a story for the photographer to capture on camera. The stylist uses props, plants, and lighting to their benefit. They use color palettes and match painted walls, wallpaper, furniture, or drapes. This person frames the display to fit on the page of a magazine. Like an interior designer, a photo stylist creates a decorated world of a room, a shelf, a table, or whatever is within the edges of the photo.

If you do not have time to run to the florist for flowers, cut a large leaf off your *Monstera*. The leaf will last for a few months. If you keep changing the water and cut a slice off the end, the stem will drink up the refreshed water. You can add more greenery if any of your houseplants can take a pruning. Maybe a long *Pothos* vine or creeping fig (*Ficus pumila*) is a good alternative for fresh greens.

BELOW LEFT: Using snapshots of life and design mixology, I am my very own living decor photo stylist. I am eager to surround myself with colorful books, decor, and plants that fuel my display engine.

BELOW: This is a sweet view of the mixology with cylinder terrariums, potted maidenhair ferns, a marble cheese board, and real, juicy strawberries. Use everyday living decor when you entertain. It is a still-life portrait that looks splendid.

## TABLE ART

The green tray full of objects sits on my coffee table year-round. It is filled with memorabilia that I have collected over time and kept adding to the tray. It became a theme of green as I added each item, and everything eventually (and unintendedly) matched the color of the original tray. I believe my unconscious eye drives my styling. I see green and out come the props that match.

There is a glass decoupage dish in the center with fern images that matches the illustrated greeting card on the left. Surprise! The pears are not real but are perfectly painted papier-mâché. The framed butterfly added another color with yellow wings seen through the clear glass. The seashell filled the last open space. You do not need to have a plan to be a styling specialist; just remember to balance and frame the space. You can start with one item, then let the objects lead you to the story.

In pulling together vignettes for this book, I discovered I have a fondness for vintage green ceramics. The Bordallo Pinheiro cabbage salad bowl was placed with the two dried artichoke heads. Bordallo Pinheiro was a Portuguese artist known for his pottery designs in the late 1800s. He founded the factory that produces these ceramics in 1885 in the city of Caldas da Rainha, where it is still in business. My dedication to the past follows me wherever I go.

What houseplant could be better in this holiday gathering? The green celebrity is a *Dracena marginata* with red-trimmed leaves. This variety of dragon plant has red-edged leaves and a striking structure. The spiked spear-shaped leaves grow from the center stem. Most people would not think to include it in a holiday display, but I like it because it is unusual.

## SEASONAL ELEMENTS

It doesn't take much for me to bring out the jingle bells! This vignette started with a red car on a tray. Memories start flooding in! What a terrific symbol of the holiday time. Straight from the tree farm is a freshly cut evergreen tree tied on the roof of an old-timey red wagon. I gathered together objects and furniture from around the house—an old red table, a deep crimson ceramic pot with a healthy *Haworthia*, and mossy-colored coconut pots filled with *Echeveria*.

## ECHEVERIA

Sweet *Echeveria*! She is the Mexican rose with a plump rosette of succulent leaves. *Echeveria* is a large genus of succulent plants native to semi-desert Mexico. This beautiful rosette form is a desert dweller. This tells us that she can live in hot, beating sun and survives in a place with little rainfall. *Echeveria* has drought-resistant adaptations.

**LIGHT:** *Echeveria* lives in the yards of Californians all over the state. How jealous am I for their sunny days? Succulents grow large and fruitful. So, bring on the sunny windows—your Mexican rose can take it.

**WATER:** Mexican rose can handle running out of water, but she doesn't need full-blown drought. When there is not available water, the plant will drop its bottom tier of leaves. If you don't want to shed any precious fleshy leaves, then give your plant a heaping drink of water and let it drain well. If you can water it before it goes bone dry, you should. It will hold its form and reward you with beautiful new circular succulent leaves.

**DESIGN MIXOLOGY:** Mexican rose can do anything, go anywhere, and look fabulous. She excels in round pots, but she often finds herself sitting in window boxes, table gardens, and bouquets of flowers. She makes everything look great.

A white porcelain commode all dressed up in white, green, and lights, the finest theme. Bright lights in every room of the home!

# COLOR INSPIRED BY GREENERY

## THE PERFECT WHITE PAINT: GREENERY'S UNIVERSAL BACKDROP

In the world of urban jungles, you will find white walls used as greenery's universal backdrop. The white does not compete with the green but instead focuses your vision on the green. Laser focus is drawn onto the plant and all its complexities. The beauty of green strips on a leaf or a structural stem's growth is illuminated on the white.

ABOVE: There is nothing fresher looking than a green leaf against a flawless white wall. How energizing that looks!

LEFT: I adore the spider plant's elegant drop of smaller spiders in midair. This plant looks great against the white wall. Add a picture that complements, and you have your snapshot.

FAR LEFT: This *Pothos* shows off its marbleized leaf pattern well in front of the calla lily print and basket of lime green Granny Smith apples. White walls help simplify the scene.

## WHITE VS. COLOR

### PINK

Could I live in a pink room? These rooms are lovely, elegant, and relaxing. They have art and plants to match their flavor. As the sun streams in and bathes the plants for the afternoon, we see how we can all thrive in a candy-sweet pink color scheme.

## BURGUNDY

LEFT: Boston fern in another room with fronds focused against burgundy paint changes the frame of mind.

## BLUE

RIGHT: Petite ponytail palm (*Beaucarnea recurvata*) has its sliver-thin cascading leaves outlined against the blue. This blue is soothing as a backdrop and picks up the spirit of the room.

BELOW: Let's jump into the blue! Chinese fan palms, *arboricola*, and *Monstera* loving the sky blues!

# III.

# RESOURCES:
## THE WORLDWIDE MARKETPLACE

**IN THIS SECTION, YOU WILL FIND VENDORS AND BLOGGERS** that will connect you with the living decor you desire! This includes flea market sites and craft fair organizers to visit, then take workshops to learn all that you can create. When you are ready to purchase, go out and peruse the brick and mortar shops in your neighborhood or click it online. Buy! Ship! Deliver!

I admit that I am an Instagram enthusiast. On Instagram, I get up close and personal with crafters around the world. We exchange ideas and collaborate. I find this inspiring and exciting. You can always direct message someone to find out about their worldwide shipping policies or inventory availability, or just ask questions about plant care.

Bring the world closer to you. Have fun and happy green travels.

Finding botanical accessories is as easy as a trip to Home Depot.

## FLEA MARKETS & CRAFT FAIRS

**Artists & Fleas**
www.artistsandfleas.com
New York, NY; Los Angeles, CA; online

**Brooklyn Flea**
www.brooklynflea.com
Brooklyn, NY

**Country Living Fair**
www.countryliving.com/country-living-fair
Nashville, TN; Rhinebeck, NY; Columbus, OH; Atlanta, GA

**Elephant's Trunk**
www.etflea.com
New Milford, CT

**Hudson River Exchange**
www.hudsonriverexchange.com
Hudson, NY

**Indie Craft Experience**
www.ice-atlanta.com
Atlanta, GA

**Indie Craft Parade**
www.makerscollective.org/indiecraftparade
Greenville, SC

**LIC Flea**
www.licflea.com
Long Island City, NY; Astoria, NY

**Renegade Craft**
www.renegadecraft.com
Austin, TX; Boston, MA; Chicago, IL; Denver, CO; Detroit, MI; London, England; Los Angeles, CA; Miami, FL; New York, NY; Portland, OR; San Francisco, CA; Seattle, WA

## RETAIL & INSTAGRAM MARKETPLACE

**Monstera Supply Co.**
Instagram: @monsterasupply.co
www.monsterasupply.co

## AIR PLANTS

**Air Plant Decor**
Instagram: @airplantdecor
www.airplantdecor.com.au
Melbourne, Australia

**Air Plant Design Studio**
Instagram: @airplantdesignstudio
www.air-plants.com

**Air Plant Hub**
Instagram: @airplanthub
www.airplanthub.com
Vacaville, CA

**Josh Rosen**
Instagram: @airplantman
www.airplantman.com
Santa Monica, CA

## BRICK & MORTAR SHOPS

**Bowood Garden & Home**
Instagram: @bowoodfarms
www.bowoodfarms.com
St. Louis, MO

**Jamali Floral & Garden Supplies**
Instagram: @jamaligarden
www.jamaligarden.com
New York, NY

**Pistils Nursery**
Instagram: @pistilsnursery
www.pistilsnursery.com
Portland, OR

**Planeta Botânico**
Instagram: @Planeta_Botanico
www.facebook.com/planetabotanico1
Brazil

**Plant**
Instagram: @plantshopyyc
www.plantterrariums.ca
Calgary, AB, Canada

**Terrain**
Instagram: @shopterrain
www.shopterrain.com
Glen Mills, PA; Westport, CT

**The ZEN Succulent**
Instagram: @thezensucculent
www.thezensucculent.com
Durham, NC; Raleigh, NC

## BLOGGERS

**City Plantz**
Instagram: @cityplantz
www.cityplantz.com
New York, NY

**Fieldnotes by Studio Plants**
Instagram: @studioplants
www.fieldnotesbystudioplants.com
Jeannie Phan
Toronto, ON, Canada

**Garden Therapy**
Instagram: @garden_therapy
www.gardentherapy.ca
Stephanie Rose
Vancouver, BC, Canada

**Urban Jungle Bloggers**
Instagram: @urbanjungleblog
www.urbanjunglebloggers.com

## BOTANICAL ILLUSTRATORS

**Autumn Von Plinsky**
Instagram: @avonplinsky
www.behance.net/avonplinsky

**Living Pattern**
Instagram: @livingpattern
www.livingpattern.net
Jenny Kiker

## GEOMETRIC TERRARIUM MAKERS

**Glass and Geometry**
Instagram: @glass_and_geometry
vk.com/glassgeometry
St. Petersburg, Russia

**MONTI**
Instagram: @montibymonti
www.montibymonti.com
London, England

## HOUSEPLANT DELIVERY SERVICE

**Bloomscape**
Instagram: @bloomscape
www.bloomscape.com
Detroit, MI

**Horti**
Instagram: @heyhorti
www.heyhorti.com
Williamsburg, NY

**Léon & George**
Instagram: @leonandgeorge
www.leonandgeorge.com
San Francisco, CA

**The Sill**
Instagram: @thesill
www.thesill.com
New York, NY

## MACRAMÉ CRAFTERS & WORKSHOPS

**Brooklyn Craft Company**
Instagram: @brooklyncraftcompany
Brooklyn, NY

**HyggeMacrame**
Instagram: @hygge_macrame
www.etsy.com/shop/
HyggeMacrameScotland
Alexandria, Ireland

## MOSS

**Artisan Moss**
Instagram: @artisanmoss
www.artisanmoss.com
Northern California

**BenettiMOSS**
Instagram: @benettimoss
www.benettihome.com
Granozzo, Italy

**Flowerbox Wall Gardens**
Instagram: @flowerboxwallgardens
www.flowerbox.us
Hoboken, NJ

**Garden Beet**
Instagram: @gardenbeet
www.gardenbeet.com
Melbourne, Australia

**Green Ecco Moss**
Instagram: @greeneccomoss
www.eccomoss.com
Russia

**Moss Acres**
www.mossacres.com
Honesdale, PA

**Moss Home Decor**
Instagram: @moss_florarium
www.moss-florarium.ru
Russia

**MossTrend**
Instagram: @mosstrend
www.mosstrend.com
Empoli, Italy

**Tennessee Wholesale Nursery**
www.tnnursery.net/moss-for-sale
Altamont, TN

## PLANTERS

**Botanica**
Instagram: @botanica.boutique
www.botanica.boutique
Stepney, SA, Australia

**Christie Lothrop**
Instagram: @madpotters
www.etsy.com/shop/MadPotters
Fallbrook, CA

**Urbio**
Instagram: @myurbio
www.myurbio.com
Oakland, CA

**WallyGro**
Instagram: @wallygro
www.wallygro.com
Kansas City, MO

## TERRARIUMS, PLANTS & WORKSHOPS

**Luludi Living Art**
Instagram: @luludilivingart
www.luludi.net
Astoria, NY

**Maria Colletti**
Instagram: @maria.colletti.399
www.green-terrariums.com
New York, NY

**Muddy Toes Terrariums**
Instagram: @muddytoesterrariums
www.muddytoesterrariums.com
Burlington, VT

**TerraLiving**
Instagram: @terraliving
www.theterraliving.com
Malacca City, Malaysia

**Terrarios & Cia**
Instagram: @terrariosecia
www.terrarios.com.br
Rio de Janeiro, Brazil

## GARDEN-INSPIRED WALLPAPER

**Meg Braff Designs**
www.megraffdesigns.com
Endura

**Milton & King**
www.miltonandking.com
Herringbone in Tree Frog Green

**York Wallcoverings**
www.yorkwall.com
Paradise Palm, pattern S02450

# INDEX

# PHOTO CREDITS

**Alcides Aguasvivas:** 72 (bottom), 74, 75, 76, 89, 98, 100 (right), 112 (right), 113, 114, 115, 116, 129, 131, 133, 135, 140, 141, 149 (right), 151

**Chad Hendricks:** 16, 66 (bottom), 87

**Lori Adams:** 4, 6, 8, 9, 11, 17, 18, 19, 22, 25 (top), 26, 28, 29, 30, 31, 32, 34, 35, 41, 43, 44, 45, 46, 49, 54, 56, 57, 58, 59, 60, 61, 62, 63, 64, 65, 67, 68, 69, 70, 71, 72 (top), 73, 77, 78, 79, 80, 81, 82, 83, 84, 85, 88, 90, 91, 92, 93, 94, 95, 96, 97, 99, 100 (left, both), 102, 104, 105, 106, 107, 108, 109, 110, 111, 112 (left), 117, 118, 119, 120, 121, 122, 123, 124, 125, 126, 127, 128, 130, 134, 136, 137, 138, 139, 142, 143, 145, 146, 147, 148, 149 (left), 150, 152, 153, 154, 155, 156 (top left), 157 (bottom), 158, 160, 176

**Meagan Rosson:** 33, 51, 52, 86

**Shutterstock:** cover (front and back), 1, 3, 13, 14, 24 (both), 25 (bottom), 37, 38, 48, 66 (top), 144, 156 (top right, bottom), 157 (top), 159

# DEDICATION

To Anthony Bourdain, host of *No Reservations* (Travel Channel) and *Parts Unknown* (CNN). His heart was an offering he gave to all of us, his life an adventure where he took us along. Thank you for teaching us to live life to the fullest and to see all the grand details uncovered layer by layer. Thank you for giving yourself. You will forever live on in my heart.

# ACKNOWLEDGMENTS

Thank you to Daniel Lawrence Hyman, my husband, my bedrock. I have accomplished many projects since we met in 2009 because I know at the end of the day the walk in the woods, the stroll on the beach, you will be by my side. Thank you for helping me when I needed help. This project challenged us. After the March 2, 2018, Nor'easter, we had no electricity for seven days and no real food in the fridge. I had spent days hauling plants and props to style urban jungle rooms to get photographed by Lori Adams at her studio and house. Two weeks later in the snow and cold, we drove a rented van up to Hopewell Junction to load several giant *Monstera*s, fiddle-leaf figs, Boston ferns, and crates of props for the long, three-hour ride home, only to empty the van again. You never complained, not one word, but at the end of the day, you said, "That's it!" I knew then we had hit bedrock! Thank you so much for helping me to create work that I am passionate doing! You and I, till the sun goes supernova . . .

Thank you to Alyssa Bluhm, my editorial project manager at the Quarto Group. What a terrific asset you are! You let me vent, you let me dream, and you let me change the table of contents every week. Thank you for your courageous unwavering editorial changes and for making this not only a terrific experience but for making this a better book than I brought to the table. I will miss our email ping-pong back and forth week after week!

Thank you to Cindy Laun, art director at the Quarto Group, for making sure that my project was in your capable hands. You watched over every detail, ensuring the love for my craft shined. With you on the project, I never worried but was very excited to see the final layout and what your team would create. Thank you!

Mark Johanson, editorial director for Cool Springs Press, thank you for making me feel how important I am to your book line and that this project means a great deal to Cool Springs Press. I really enjoyed our professional discussions and how you assisted me along the ups and downs of writing a manuscript. You are a terrific publishing professional. Thank you for signing book number two.

Thank you to the fantastic contributing angels that I met on Instagram! It all started with Christie Lothrop of @MadPotters and her exceptional cement pot designs. Your energy and positive spirit is beautiful. You jumped right in while moving your entire life to Southern California to live your succulent dreams. Thank you for sharing knowledge of your craft and photos. Then, as if that weren't enough, when I needed some local photography help, you served up your photographer of @MadPotters publicity photos, Alcides Aquasvivas, co-owner of Pix-i Graphx of Kearny, New Jersey. Alcides, photographer extraordinaire, said yes with eager delight to explore the world of plant photography. Thank you, Al—you are simply a pleasure to work with and I hope we get the chance to collaborate again. Thank you to Cathleen Aquasvivas for coming along for the ride and instinctively propping the food so deliciously. What a dynamic duo!

Amelie Segrestan, @MyLittleGreens, friend of Christie, boldly came forward and asked to be part of our Instagram plant parade. You and your photographer, Chad Hendricks, spent hours making a perfect New York moment. Well, did you surprise me with a fabulous array of foliage basking against an urban skyline. Thank you for providing that NYC vibe for the author's East Coast origins.

Now, we come to Brooklyn and Mac, the real stars of *Living Decor*, the wonderful impish cats of Meagan Rosson and Jensen Gardner of @Plant_Lady_is_the_New_Cat_Lady. Thank you for loaning your fabulous cats, those darling little rascals always nipping at your houseplants. Thank you, Jensen, for spending hours waiting on those felines to cooperate. I just love it!

Everything happens in Brooklyn! These people added marvelous ideas and photographs of how they use plants as living decor. I thank you for joining me on this journey. I wish for you all a prosperous 2019 and beyond.

Well, not exactly everything happens in Brooklyn. Lori Adams, photographer on *Terrariums: Gardens under Glass*, was my first choice to bring an artistic eye and flare to this book. Your deep dedication to your craft is in every photo. As you look through your camera lens, I know each time you waited for the light, you balanced on the staircase, and followed me around clicking away while I poured soil in glass. You made my actions and my room designs an artistic focus. Thank you for working so hard during those days in cold, snowy Hudson Valley. Thank you also to Judith Kepner Rose for allowing us to the use of your Rabbit Sculpture, an added surprise. Thank you, Lori, for traveling on location to Mary Moeller's home to create more snapshot moments! The cow shot (page 150) is pure gold. I wish you years of prosperous photo gigs and successful show sales. Be well, my friend, and live long and prosper!

# ABOUT THE AUTHOR

Maria Colletti, author of *Terrariums: Gardens Under Glass*, is a traveling workshop instructor and modern indoor gardener. Maria teaches terrarium-making classes throughout the New York metro area. She also sells her custom-made terrariums at street fairs and flea markets such as Nyack Street Fair or Bronxville Street Sale. Her signature glass globe, the Katie, has gravel, sand, seashells, and terrarium plants or air plants.

She currently teaches at the New York Botanical Garden, changing her classes from season to season, featuring topics from Living Decor to Tropical Rainforest with Orchids. She teaches teambuilding and party workshops for the NYBG's Adult Education department as well. Maria has spent most of her adult life working at NYBG, starting right out of college and later spending thirteen amazing years as the store manager of Shop in the Garden until 2017. The wildly successful retail store on the garden property is where she perfected her decor skills and had every plant and supply available to create her signature designs.

In spring 2017, Maria started a two-year working experience with Terrain of Westport in Connecticut, the unbelievable home and garden store from Urban Outfitters and Anthroplogie. Terrain is terrarium nirvana, houseplant heaven on earth, and gardening personified. Maria learned all she could from the remarkable gardeners at the store. Always a journey worth traveling . . .

Maria lectures with accompanying workshops at library programs for Westbury Library and West Hempstead Library. She was an artisan speaker at the Sands Point and New Canaan Garden Club monthly meeting and the wonderful spring luncheon at the Rye Yacht Club. As mentioned in this book, she presents workshops at the Bartow-Pell Mansion Museum in the conservatory room. In 2016, she was featured presenter at *Country Living* magazine's fair in Rhinebeck, New York. You can hear her radio interview by NPR's *You Bet Your Garden* host, Mike McGrath.

Maria's work, books, and terrarium tips have been featured in the *Washington Post*, *Toronto Star*, *San Diego Union Tribune*, and other newspapers around the country. She has been published in *Cottages & Bungalows*, *Country Gardens*, and has had her designs featured online by HGTV and Architectural Digest. She was dubbed the "terrarium savant" in online article for *Edible Manhattan*. The queen of green!

Maria began her career as a terrace gardener on the rooftops of Manhattan. Then, she loved working for a plantscaping firm as a caretaker for large atriums, such as the Guggenheim Museum. Maria has degrees in horticulture and anthropology.